I dedicate my autobiography to my beloved husband and son, Alan and David, now with our Father God; to my ever loving daughter Mandy, and grandson David Alan, both my supportive backbone throughout the years; and also to Tally, Mandy's much-loved canine partner.

Chapter 1

The birth of a second daughter in 1927 was a great disappointment to my father George. I had been destined to be named Vivian George after him, so I had to be called Vivian Georgina. Daphne was the name of my older sister. My mother had really only wanted two children, but the third child born after me, very fortunately for my mother, was a son. His name was Colin. My father was immensely proud of him.

Both my parents were strong. They were survivors. Their suffering had been great, like so many others who went through the agonies of separation and emotional deprivation during the First World War. They met on Hastings sea front during the second year of the war when George, who was on leave, offered my mother Grace half of his precious bar of chocolate. They later became engaged, then were kept apart during those awful years of death and destruction.

My parents were a striking couple. Father's grand-father was Irish. George was an exceptionally handsome man with his jet-black hair, deep blue eyes and his ready smile. He was also naturally very muscular and athletic. Grace was of small stature, her fairness a sharp contrast to that of her beloved husband. Her hair in her earlier years seemed to me to be of a gorgeously golden colour; her complexion was fair, while her hazel-coloured eyes had a constant sparkle. My mother's spreading smile would always welcome those to whom she was speaking, even when she became involved in one of those rare visits paid by George's two sisters.

George, determined to serve his beloved country, had volunteered for service in the army aged seventeen, having lied about his age. Early in 1915, a few months before meeting my mother, he had volunteered to switch to the Royal Air Force, despite being informed that the average life expectancy for a pilot was just three weeks. George, in the firm belief that the air force would be instrumental in leading his country to an early victory, was prepared to lay down his life for King and Country. Fortunately for both my parents, the switch was never made. My father reck-oned at the time that the reason behind his rejection was most probably due to his total lack of piloting experience.

Armistice was declared in 1918, and George emerged richer by a Military Medal. While in army service, he had succeeded 'beyond the call of duty' in rescuing troops, many of them his friends. During one such rescue, he and his fellow soldiers were temporarily blinded, buried beneath the rubble during a bombing attack. My father also survived Gallipoli. I think that the memory of those British landing boats being blown up by gunfire stayed with him for the rest of his life. Many were drowned as they struggled through the sea to reach the hostile shore while laden down with backpacks, but many hapless men also lost their lives under the merciless fusillade from the Turkish gunners on the heights above. It is my belief that those wartime memories continued to haunt my father until the end of his days.

George was a man who kept his painful thoughts to himself. However, I remember very clearly, during the commencement of the Second World War in 1939 when I was eleven, him muttering to me while on one of our walks together: 'They never had a chance.' It was a moment of rare confidence. Intuitively I knew he was still thinking about Gallipoli and those other painful experiences he went through during the First World War. He did not allow himself many times of such closeness.

During the early months of the Second World War, my intensely patriotic 'for God and Country' father and I were watching an aerial dogfight from our garden. Suddenly the German plane descended, flames streaming from the tail. I felt frightened; was someone burning to death? A parachute emerged. My father's eyes filled with tears. I must have looked puzzled, for surely the pilot had survived. It was then my father whispered, 'There should have been two.'

To my father, and to countless others, the promise had been made: that the First World War was to be 'the war to end all wars'. He surely saw that dead German as being a member of a loving family unit, such as our own, who would be mourned over by his parents. My father was normally never one to display any emotion. Dear Father, I have never forgotten those tears.

My mother was sensitive and loving. Her parents, both orthodox Jews, were refugees from Vilna in Poland. Hard-working, they lived in the East End of London, remaining poor throughout their life. There were thirteen children, one who died in infancy, and my mother was the eleventh. At her school, where Yiddish was spoken, she became both the games and swimming captain. Her parents understood little English, but my mother made it her duty to master the language, and later sought out elocution lessons, paying for them by work undertaken during the school holidays. She gained a scholarship to an excellent day school in London, but despite personal pleas from her teacher, her parents felt that they could not afford the extra clothes required, nor yet the loss of income from a working daughter. This is probably why, after she married my father, she insisted that a first-class education was an absolute priority for her own three children. She was of an independent nature, and later became a suffragette.

Even as a small child I felt saddened that, for some reason, which I failed to fully understand, we lacked the presence of grandparents from both sides of the family. I really envied those friends of mine who received visits and gifts from their loving grandparents on a regular basis; mine seemed to really dislike us.

When my mother became engaged to my father, initially only Clare, one of her sisters, remained in contact with her. Later, other members of her family – her brothers, Sam and David, and her older sister, Mary – became part of our extended family. Clare was a constant visitor, and our ever-loving aunt. She always arrived at our home carrying a large bag of sweets for each one of us, along with a little pocket money. She remained single during her lifetime; we were her much-loved family. Sam, my mother's older brother, emigrated to America in his early twenties; there he became wealthy as the finance manager of several large successful business organisations. Uncle Sam also had some connection with a similar British firm, and would visit England every year and would stay with us in our home. Daphne, Colin and I would always welcome his visits; we each would receive a small gift of money before he returned to America.

Our Jewish grandfather refused to recognise his married daughter and her family, while his wife, our grandmother, visited us just the once, some months after the death of her husband. My mother told us her father was a very good man. He would say prayers over the dying, comfort the mourners over the grave in all weathers and, in so doing, died of pneumonia when I was aged four. As I grew older, I was saddened not to have met him.

My father's family had not a kind word to say to the alien Jewish woman who had stolen their beloved George. To them, marrying a woman of the Jewish faith was totally unacceptable. We never met his father; there was a total refusal to maintain any form of contact, despite all my mother's efforts. George's mother, Ruth, visited us once after her husband's death, acting as though she was royalty. Petite, and dressed in black, she treated my mother like a wayward child, who should be placed out of sight and certainly out of mind. Father's two sisters visited on several occasions, but never had a kind word to say to my mother or to us, her children. There were never any gifts or birthday cards for any of us. The visits remained formal in nature, despite all my mother's efforts to soothe the situation with her kind nature. The intrusion of Jewish blood into their family was clearly not acceptable. It caused me puzzlement as a child; surely Jesus, God's Son, was born into a Jewish family. I failed to understand just why Jewish people were not liked by some Christian people.

'At least you do not look like a Jew,' were the first words said to my mother by my father's oldest sister on her first visit. Aged four years, I was standing by my mother's side, holding her hand. My mother had flaxen curly hair that glistened gold in the sunlight, a very fair complexion, rosy cheeks and hazel-coloured sparkling eyes. Mother made no reply, while I stood clutching her hand protectively. I always tried to protect my mother against the emotional pain following those visits by my father's family; I felt that my role was both to comfort and shield her mind from any such pain. I would always stay by her side, interrupting their conversation with what was probably interpreted as childish questioning: it did, however, seem to work. My mother would continue to smile as we clutched hands. My mother was a first-class cook, and the meals offered to her guests were always scrumptious. Second helpings were always enjoyed.

During the Second World War, I often pondered over those words spoken by my father's older sister, so clearly expressing the deep dislike of Jewish people. I was fearful that should the Nazis ever succeed in invading England, she would betray our Jewish blood to them. There were times when I became desperately afraid for my parents, my sister and brother Daphne and Colin, and myself. Although the Nazis had an evil reputation, there was also an element of anti-Semitic sentiment that ran through our community. My mother warned me repeatedly never to mention our ancestry to any of my friends, whether within school or church.

I did, however, break my promise. I became friends with a Jewish refugee from Germany. Gustav, along with his mother and his brother, Adolf, were taken into the home of their uncle, a close neighbour of our family. His father had died in a concentration camp. Gustav and I became really good friends, and we certainly enjoyed each other's company. We spent time both talking and walking together; proudly I let him know that my mother was Jewish and that her parents had also been refugees, having fled from Vilna in Poland in earlier years. I hope that this information made Gustav feel less alone in life. Later he told me that while still in Germany, he had joined the Hitler Youth. Once his ancestry was revealed he was forcefully ejected from the organisation. I failed to understand why he had even considered entering the Nazi youth movement, but I believe he had joined while still at a very young age. My mother supported the refugees, and we were all taken on family outings together. Gustav and later his younger brother, Adolf, decided to join the armed forces three years after the Second World War had commenced; Gustav was just eighteen years of age. He promised to come back home again, and visit me, but he never returned. He died abroad while fighting to serve the country he had grown to love. I grieved, not only for the loss of my friend, but also for his family. Adolf returned home safely once the war was over. It was for his mother a blessed relief. She had lost two members of her family because of the Nazis: her husband died while enclosed within a German concentration camp, and her eldest son. Their surname was *Itler*, which brought a wry

smile to our faces whenever our family thought about
them. My parents did their utmost to support the grief-
stricken family. Eventually both Adolf and his mother
moved abroad, and sadly we lost contact.

My parents, although they were not of the Christian
faith, always insisted that we children attend the local
Sunday school and then church as their ages advanced.
There, all children were offered a welcoming friendship.
My mother always maintained her belief in the Jewish
faith, while my father was a Unitarian – Unitarians see
Jesus as a prophet but believe that God is a single person,
not the Father, Son and Holy Spirit, and as such are
outside conventional religion.

I still have a vivid memory of walking down Acton
High Street after my mother had a major operation at our
local hospital. She was very weary. We passed an undertaker's office, but at that time I did not understand what
being an undertaker meant. The window was decorated
with a glorious display of flowers. I desperately wanted
to buy her something that she could not afford. Yearning
to please her, I whispered '*One day I will buy you some
flowers just like them.*' It was not until many months had
passed by that I understood just why such a long silence
had followed those words of mine.

Later in life, my mother told me how she had always craved the stimulus of some kind of employment during her married life, but even before the birth of my sister Daphne, my Victorian-like father refused to give sanction. No wife of his would undertake work. However, during the Second World War, Mother became a much-valued member of the Women's Royal Voluntary Service. She became deeply committed to the care of the Belgian refugees who swarmed into the country, and was the first to organise a follow-up of these troubled people who had been billeted in our area.

I can still recall her deep anger and active concern when she found that one young woman had been allocated shelter within a house where the sole occupant, a male, demanded nightly services, forcing the refugee to share his bedroom. How fiercely my mother managed that re-allocation. However, her fear that a pregnancy could ensue was not realised; my mother kept a kindly watchful eye over that young woman in the following months, ensuring that her privacy was protected.

My mother also took a long-term interest in two Belgian teenagers, Charles and his sister Regina, who were always made welcome in our home. They were billeted close to us. Both were orphans, their parents having been killed by the German invaders. Charles and Regina often accompanied us on our family treats together. Visits to Kew Gardens were a special favourite, as well as times spent in the local swimming pool. Mother bought Regina a really nice swimming costume for her birthday, so her swimming was always enjoyed.

My father was a Home Guard during the war period, and he took the work very seriously, although his serving time was limited to a certain extent, as he was still in full-time employment. George was the chief engineer employed on a national basis within Nestlé, the chocolate manufacturing firm. My father's return home from work was always welcomed by his three expectant children. We enjoyed our visits to Nestlé, along with our mother, and we always arrived back home along with a bag of delicious chocolates.

I looked like my father in many ways, although as a small child I was always small and skinny. This used to worry my mother, who always cooked marvellous meals, even during the war period. Despite my size, I always ate a lot, and enjoyed all of her cooking. Her feelings were deeply hurt during my examination by the visiting School Medical Officer, who told my mother that I was suffering from malnutrition, while my plump sister was said to have 'excellent nutrition'. My poor mother was devastated, feeling obliged to believe the doctor. Those were the days when the doctor's word was sacrosanct and never questioned. In vain I was given fattening foods, but I still remained skinny. My mother never forgot that incident. Despite my constant enjoyment of her scrumptious meals, she continued to ensure that I was always offered a second helping of food. Daphne was envious: her food intake remained under my mother's constant observation. A second helping, unless it was of vegetables, was never permitted; nevertheless, my sister always remained plump, unable to cope with netball and tennis during our school life together. In her earlier years she was deemed to be the best swimmer in her class; sadly even swimming had to be put aside during her senior days at school.

I started my school life in a little local Catholic convent school, at the age of four. I can still vividly remember the penny given to me by my mother, required to get a little black child one rung further up her ladder to heaven. My mother had few to spare, but she offered to give me a penny every day. Some weeks later, when she came to collect me, she asked one of the teacher nuns if she could see my small wooden ladder which had been set up within my class. Alas, my little black child had advanced no further up the ladder: her feet were still on the bottom rung. Mother was bewildered for a short time but soon discerned the answer. Sadly, Vivian had sinned. The pennies had been spent upon tubes of fizzy lemon sweets sold by the nuns.

I felt guilty for a long time afterwards. I wondered: would I ever get to heaven? I had committed a sin. I suffered silently for many days, until I was comforted by Sister Mary. She was the oldest among those teaching nuns; she found me one day crying in the corner of the classroom, after being mocked by some of my classmates. My sinful actions had been witnessed by some of the other pupils. Sister Mary not only assured me of forgiveness, once my cry to be forgiven during prayer time had been made; she also gently but firmly remonstrated with my classmates. In consequence I was left in peace. The matter was never referred to again.

Sister Mary became my friend, one who would always help me in times when I perceived trouble. For some unknown reason, I was a particularly sensitive child. I lacked confidence in myself, and initially failed to react when bullying techniques were employed by those who enjoyed being assertive in nature. I was always selected as a target by bullies. It was Sister Mary who taught me how to respond in speech; how to express my feelings both clearly and without anger. Slowly over the time spent within that convent, my confidence improved under the loving care of that nun. In retrospect, the incident relating to my acquisition of those fizzy lemon sweets had its proven value. It was through Sister Mary that I learnt to express myself definitively without resorting to tears. Thank you, Sister Mary, you are not forgotten.

Eventually Mother managed to persuade my father to invest in a house. My father had by that time received an honoured promotion to that of chief engineer on an international basis within Nestlé. In consequence, a house was purchased in Acton, north-west London, that was only a few minutes' walk from the Haberdashers' Aske's Girls' School, which was deemed right for both my sister and me. It had a very good academic record, and was known for its fine sporting activities. There was a playing field, and a swimming pool adjoining the school, which was for the sole use of its pupils. The school my brother was to go to was not too far away.

During the start of my school life, I lived in a dream world of my own creation. I read many books about missionary work in Africa; the need by many of its poorer inhabitants for both food and medical care. The country fascinated me. I came to believe that God meant me to be a missionary doctor, caring for all those hungry little babies, perhaps the hungriest babies in the world. Indulging in my dreams, lessons often passed me by, and my early school reports were certainly not encouraging. I did, however, manage to make some friends in my new school, and also enjoyed some of the lessons, especially English and history. I had real difficulties, though, with my reasoning abilities in mathematics, and it was not until later years that this was resolved.

I formed one special friendship with a shy, clever girl called Dilys. She was often made form captain, an honour never ever accorded to me. Unfortunately for her, we both looked alike from the rear. We both had thick brown curly hair with a glint of gold that stood out like a bush from our heads. When I became engaged many years later, my fiancé called me 'Fuz Wuz'. As we were both of a similar build, Dilys was often reprimanded when I spoke out of turn, but then the mistake would be revealed when she turned to face her accuser. My untidy self, bright blue eyes and ruddy complexion, were in total contrast to her paler intellectual face and consistently neat appearance.

All my teachers despaired during those earlier years of my school life. I remained a dreamer. Having a strong imagination, I believe that most of my thoughts remained in the missionary fields of Africa; I was there daily, caring for those little needy African babies and ministering to all their basic needs. For me, it seemed like the will of God.

It was only owing to the intervention of a teacher that my schoolwork dramatically improved, although it wasn't until I started to think seriously about the subjects I should take for my General Certificate examination. It was a vitally important year. By that time I had changed my missionary allegiance for Africa to that of China, having become enraptured with the mystique of the East. A talk had been given during the Sunday service at my local church by a missionary from China who had just arrived home on leave.

While studying for my General Certificate and matriculation examination, I had made up my mind to learn Mandarin, and managed to borrow some books from the public library. These were obtained with some difficulty by the librarian, and I was allowed to keep them for a prolonged period. I did not tell my parents that I had decided to master the Mandarin language. I studied seriously till late every night, to the amazement and joy of my parents, both believing that I was concentrating on my examinations.

My maths teacher Miss Skelensky changed all that. She was a Polish lady who seemed quite distressed by my constantly poor performance in class, and most probably the anticipated failures in the coming O level certificate. She used her large bust like the prow of a ship, wending its way through our closely sited desks. There she inspected our work. I dreaded her coming, for she was always armed with a red-ink pen. My school exercise book for mathematics was scored with red crosses and rarely a tick: the subject was totally incomprehensible, absolutely out of this world. On one never to be forgotten occasion, she took me aside: 'Vivian, what do you want to be when you leave school?'

'A medical missionary, a doctor, Madam. I am trying to learn Mandarin.' I looked solemnly up into her face. 'The books from the library are very good, but it took a really long time for those library people to find the right books for me, and it is such a very difficult language to learn. I am working really hard, and it takes hours and hours of my time, but I believe God wants me to learn Mandarin. I am going to be a missionary ... a missionary doctor ... in China.'

A deep sigh emanated from Miss Skelensky. Her large bosom swayed tremulously, always a sign of her concern. Her hand grasped mine.

'Vivian, don't you realise that in order to be a doctor, a medical missionary, you have to pass both your school and your General Certificate examinations. You could not even be awarded with a matriculation certificate. You have never passed a mathematics examination since you have been in my class, not once. Are you good in your other subjects?'

'Only English literature and history,' was my despondent reply.

Blue eyes looked into mine. It came to me then that her eyes were gentle and kind and that she really seemed to care. She was the first teacher ever to talk to me seriously, as though I really mattered to her; that I was actually a pupil of importance in her life.

'You must get up to matriculation level in mathematics, French, the sciences, as well as in your favourite subjects. I know just the girl to teach you mathematics at home. She is now in the sixth form, taking her A levels. You must speak to your mother. I am sure that Dorothy would be glad to get some extra pocket money. You have now just enough time ahead of you to catch up with all your subjects, but only if you put your heart and mind into achieving that miracle.'

The memory of those words marked a turning point in my life during the following months. Even now, some seventy years later, I can visualise that rotund figure, the bulbous bust, and the face bending down over me, neatly framed by the thickness of grey hair twirled into a bun at the back of her head. I put Mandarin aside, and bought a marvellous book entitled *Hugo's Teach Yourself French*. Painstakingly I perused it chapter by chapter. I enjoyed the challenge. The mathematics coaching went well. Dorothy, who later was to become a teacher, was exceptionally patient with her odd young pupil. My understanding of geometry, algebra and arithmetic advanced steadily once I had put my mind to the diligent study of each subject. The mysteries of the sciences were explored by learning a few basic principles. I found to my delight that I really enjoyed biology, while English literature and history remained my shield and anchor. My mother managed to obtain a tutor who somehow managed to give me guidance in the learning of French, while my personal study of the Sciences enabled me to come to terms with the subjects. The end-of-term report stated to my delighted parents that 'Vivian has now returned to the world around her'.

The Second World War was in progress, and the air-raid sirens had started just as I had left home for school on the morning that the dreaded O levels began. I should have returned back home, but I disobeyed orders. I had my priorities. I prayed hard for inspiration. The hymn at the early morning assembly was clearly meant for me. I joined in with solemn gusto.

Come Holy Ghost our souls inspire,
And lighten with celestial fire.

We could clearly hear 'doodlebugs', the flying bombs, from the safety of our school basement cloakroom, which had been cleverly converted into an air-raid shelter. It was there that we took our school certificate examinations. Clare, one of the cleverest girls in the class, was highly strung, and started to cry while trying to write, and tears plopped steadily over her work. Sadly, her results reflected her agitation. I sympathised, and wished dearly on her behalf that something could have been done to enable her to have a second chance. Other girls shed tears along with her in sympathy following the finish of that examination. Clare remained distraught; she could not be comforted.

We were all upset, but somehow my kind teacher's advice stayed with me and I seemed to have become inspired when initially scanning the sheet. It was uncanny. I could actually understand the problems presented by the algebra paper. Following my teacher's instructions, I tackled the easiest ones first, and so built up some measure of confidence. I was lucky. I ignored all the noises made by those threatening doodlebugs. They only affected me when our desks shook, but even that fear passed. The stillness that momentarily followed was strangely soothing. My mathematics coach had sown the seed well. My application to *Hugo's Teach Yourself French* stood me in excellent stead in my French examination, as did the cramming of those scientific principles.

Matriculation was awarded. I obtained good credits in all the relevant subjects, all thanks to a compassionate teacher. I was a happier child. I was perhaps more at ease with myself in the sixth form than at any other time within my school life.

My feet were at last firmly on the ground. I decided that a nursing career was the only option open to me. I think it fair to point out that in those earlier periods, when women did not have equal status to men, professional training for women in medicine was of a very low priority and female students were certainly not welcomed into that male-dominated world. Over the following years, the door opened slowly to women, but only to those with the highest of academic achievements. Even three very clever girls in my school who were awarded excellent grades in their A levels failed to be accepted to study medicine. My parents had struggled with school fees for three children, and at that time only men were eligible for educational grants. It seemed very unfair. My prospects of becoming what I wanted to be most in the world seemed to be extremely bleak. A training course in nursing seemed to be the only solution. I decided that after achieving the final State Registration in Nursing, which would take me three years of training, I would become a midwife, and attach myself to the China Inland Mission.

My father expressed a great anger at my decision. His deep blue eyes directed towards me expressed the rage smouldering beneath the surface. It spilt out like lava from an erupting volcano. Nursing, in his opinion, was for the less-educated women, whose lowly duties consisted in keeping both the ward and the patients clean and fed, while administering medication prescribed by the doctor. Only later, once he had seen me work, would his opinion of nursing duties become updated.

While still at school, my full attention was brought to bear upon my chosen subjects, those being English literature along with English, history and scripture. The latter was not an accepted A level within my school, but special studies in scripture were arranged. Finally I spent only one year in the sixth form, deciding not to waste further time in completion of the A levels, as I felt they would be of no advantage to me in nursing. Only success in matriculation was essential for entry into nurse training within a London teaching hospital. It seemed vitally important to proceed with the important business of life outside my school; of ministering to Chinese children and to take my entrance into the wide world.

Chapter 2

University College Hospital in London was a large and imposing building. However, once inside a ready welcome was always ensured. It was modern in its concept of nurse tuition, being the first in England to initiate a 'Preliminary Training School', or 'PTS', for nursing students. Throughout the three-year training, leading to the State Registration, each nurse returned regularly to the PTS for around six weeks, and during those training and learning periods we were given complete freedom from ward duties. It was a brilliant innovation, and training was undertaken within the hospital building itself, which meant that no travelling was involved. Nurses could study and also relax during the evening while within the PTS class situation. For us trainee nurses these six weeks were a time when learning could be enjoyed within a stress-free environment. It gave us all a period of time for further friendships to be made. It was for me a time of enjoyment.

'It was the best of times; it was the worst of times. It was the spring of hope; the spring of despair.' I was so fortunate in that a close schoolfriend of mine named Christina started her nursing training along with me in 1946. We felt we had both the best, and also the worst, before us. We needed each other, and had many a laugh together while comforting each other during our daily trials and tribulations. Those three years in training were not always easy. Together we managed to surmount those waves of despair, to laugh when the clouds above us seemed darkly threatening during those times spent within the wards.

The depths of our ignorance were abysmal. We laughed at all our mistakes in order to survive the sharpness of some of the sisters' tongues. One young nurse in her early training was asked to sterilise the ward thermometers. This she achieved by boiling them for a full five minutes. A shattering of glass followed, and the ward sister was clearly not amused. The ward's supply of thermometers had to be fully replaced. A patient with an acutely painful ear infection was admitted; she confessed to being severely constipated. One of my friends was asked by the ward sister to administer a suppository, a medicated plug designed to be inserted into the rectum, the terminal part of the large intestine. One was stuck gently into each ear; the patient willingly complied. This seemed the logical place to a young trainee nurse. However, I think one of my actions achieved some of the loudest laughter within our set of nurses. Giggles reverberated around the lunch table when I told the story.

During a grand round, when the visiting professor of surgery, who was also the surgeon to the royal family, was surrounded by his admiring entourage of doctors and medical students, I had responded to a patient's call for a bedpan. Only later did I learn that it was taboo to administer a bedpan during that renowned consultant's visit. My second offence on that momentous occasion was slipping on the floor in my hurry to return to the sluice, and empty the bedpan down the ward toilet. It fell to the ward floor, clattering over the tiled surface. Mesmerised, I watched it follow that learned dignitary, depositing its entire contents neatly over his shoes. I was only comforted when the consultant smiled at me during the time when his shoes were being changed. Forgiveness was mine.

Another time, I was left alone by night for a short interval while the senior nurse departed for a meal. It was the usual practice that only one senior and one junior nurse was allocated to each ward by night. One elderly confused male patient made his way out of the ward and wandered downstairs, while I had to take my time in attending to another elderly patient's intimate needs. Unfortunately, he made an entry into the very strict night sister's office. She was known to employ bullying techniques with the more junior staff. That particular incident was reported to matron, and went down on my final report. According to her, I had been grossly negligent. I realised that the results could have been cata-strophic for that somewhat confused elderly patient; he could have fallen down outside the ward, and possibly suffered from a fractured bone, or a flesh injury.

Christina and I remained a mutual support and comfort to each other. Alone while in training we possibly could not have survived very long, as both of us were very sensitive to the needs not only of each other, but also of those of all our patients. Just a few trainees left within the earlier months of training, unable to cope with the prob-lems experienced by some patients, seen daily in the wards; another felt that she could not tolerate the strict discipline imposed by some of the senior nurses and sisters.

During my early training, a kindly ward sister desig-nated another older probationer to 'look after me' as I was thought to be too timid in nature. I think that having let one of my patients wander out of the ward during the night had severely jolted my confidence. Ann, the older nurse, had previously served in the Forces; she was of a resilient yet gentle character. The two of us were set to work together in a very busy ward under a German sister who was efficient and kind towards her patients and nursing staff alike, and she was particularly gentle with those nurses on probation. Her son was a houseman – or junior doctor as they are known now – who also worked within the hospital. He was very popular with the students as he was always happy to impart information. His mother was the only sister known to hold teaching rounds for her nursing staff. She gave praise when she felt it to be justified, and encouragement to those in need of help and advice. Sister's teaching procedures always succeeded in raising the confidence of her ward nurses who were still in training.

A lovable little girl died quite unexpectedly on her return to that sister's ward following an emergency procedure in the operating theatre. She had received stitches for a serious cut on her abdomen, and she had lost so much blood that she had to receive a transfusion. The poor little girl's mother had left her alone in the home for just a few moments in order to post a letter. In her absence, the little girl had decided to play with a large carving knife she had found in a kitchen drawer. It seemed that as she was playing, the child had tripped and fallen onto the sharp edge of the knife. Despite every effort made to preserve the little girl's life, she died on the following day. The cause of death was determined to be that of profound shock following rapid blood loss. The child's name was Edwina. It was both the first and the last time I was to see a sister weep. Her death was so unexpected. We had all cared for little Edwina; she had been such a brave little girl, one always ready with a smile.

Deidre was another child who I remember well. She lived along with Evelyn, her mother, who was serving as a medical missionary in Africa. Evelyn had been given compassionate leave from her missionary work because Sara, her elderly mother, had only just survived a sudden attack of pneumonia and needed her daughter's comforting presence at home with her in England. Evelyn was her only child. Once she had returned to health, grandmother Sara had come to worry about her grandchild. Deidre, aged two, was a pale-faced, rather lethargic child, one who was apparently unwilling to play with other small children in the local park. Deidre always complained of feeling tired. A visit to the local doctor had been arranged, and I was informed that his initial diagnosis had been that of anaemia and malnutrition, which was confirmed following various investigatory blood tests. Deidre had quickly been admitted to hospital, and the family doctor's diagnosis had been confirmed. Apparently the mother had also worked as a midwife during her time abroad, while also undertaking the missionary work. Evelyn was a widow, and while she performed her missionary work, the daily care of little Deidre had been left to a kindly African lady who, following the local custom, had fed the child on a diet mainly of milk and bread. Apparently it had not been realised that the sole dietary combination of milk and bread on a daily basis was totally inadequate for a growing child. Evelyn was distraught and ridden with guilt. I managed to comfort her, and reassured her that vitamin and iron administration, along with a continuing healthy intake of food, would resolve the problem in time. The sudden illness of the grandmother that brought her back to England, and her concerns regarding her grandchild, had undoubtedly preserved young Deidre's health, perhaps even her life. I understand that the young child remained in good health following her discharge from hospital, and I was relieved to learn from the local press that mother and daughter remained in England, and that Evelyn became married several months later to a local doctor. I shall never know for certain, but I believe Deidre's illness meant that they never returned to missionary service in Africa. Sometimes, especially in cases such as this one, I yearned to have some feedback from the family doctor concerning my patients' ongoing lives. I had let myself become fond of Deidre while she was a patient. In time I forced myself to accept that all such contact was on a temporary basis and that I never may know the final outcome.

Along with me, about twenty-five probationers had commenced training. Some casualties were inevitable, although the majority made it through. However, for some, the stresses and strains seemed quite difficult to manage. Unhappiness could so often be followed by ill health. Most of the trainees were in their late teens or early twenties. One of my special friends left when she became pregnant; there was no allowance for unwed expectant mothers in our ranks. During my training time, another young nurse caught poliomyelitis while serving within the children's ward. Once out of the acute respiratory failure stage, she was nursed within the private wing; initially we were not allowed to visit, because of the fear of cross infection. She became partially paralysed. An older friend of mine caught tuberculosis though she did recover. Another attempted suicide. Later, two others decided to leave and get married. A close ex-Forces friend of mine decided to leave as the emotional pain she experienced while watching others suffer was too unbearable. During our three-year training period, Christina and I would meet during our off-duty periods. Through all those hard times, Christina and I consoled each other; we were so blessedly fortunate in having such an enduring friendship throughout our training together, which gave each of us both support and strength.

On night duty, I was sometimes troubled by a slim blonde night sister, who took pleasure in making unexpected visits to the wards and persecuting the tired and inexperienced probationers. She would always find fault with our performance. Woe betide any nurse caught entertaining a houseman in the kitchen with a cup of tea or coffee. Many of my friends developed a strategy for coping with her visits, but that sister's sharp criticisms during my early days of training meant that I dreaded her unannounced inspections. Later as I became more experienced, I learnt to deal with those feelings, and not to bow down to her bullying techniques. It was only then that Sister's unexpected entry into the ward during the night time became greeted with a ready smile.

One evening, while serving on a medical ward, I was asked to 'special' John, an eighteen-year-old soldier. 'Special' meant that I was given sole care of him, and had no other patient responsibilities. The senior nurse on duty could always be called if John deteriorated in any way and, if not available, the night sister could be approached. My patient had managed to become infected with encephalitis, an inflammation of the brain tissue, while serving abroad. He was barely conscious and could not speak. However, I learnt to anticipate his every need by the way that he flickered his eyes, by his strange cries, and even in the uncoordinated movements of his hands. I came to love both him and his widowed mother. John was her only child. During one late night his respirations suddenly began to wax and wane. He had short periods when he hyperventilated, followed by times in which he scarcely seemed to breathe. It was during that period that I sensed the sad reality: John was being approached by the harbinger of death. I realised that both his mother and the sister ought to be informed immediately. However, John's hands gripped me tightly while he struggled with his breathing. His eyes flickered, then looked directly into mine. It seemed as if we had known each other forever. Suddenly he smiled at me, his first conscious recognition of me since his admission to hospital.

'Hold me,' he whispered, his brown eyes fixed firmly upon mine. 'Please don't leave me ... *you must not leave me now* ... hold me ... hold me ... hold me close ... close ... *never ... leave ... me ... hold me now.*'

These were the first words spoken by my patient while in the ward. John continued to clutch my hands, his eyes fixed upon mine. I knew I could not leave his side, not to call for medical help, nor make a request for the presence of his mother. It was too late and there was too little time. Calling for help would only have distressed my patient. I held him to me, rocking him gently, a mother with her child. His respirations steadied, and his body relaxed against mine. Suddenly the stress lines slipped away from his face. John looked young again. At eighteen years old, he was ready for his next adventure. His fingers tightened upon mine, then relaxed as he uttered his last words. They were so faint that I had to lean closely over him in order to hear.

'Goodbye ... see you again one day ... my love to Mum.' Then he smiled, but not at me.

John died in my arms. Numbed with grief, I allowed myself the luxury of tears, thanking God that John's demise had been so unutterably peaceful. I wept for the widowed mother, for she had lost her only son. It was then that I composed myself, knowing that I would have to contact the dreaded night sister. Inevitably she would find fault with everything I had done, even perhaps in allowing my patient to die. This was during the period of time when I was still fearful of that woman. Carefully I checked all my charts. All the recordings were neatly presented. John's bed had been screened from the rest of the ward. I knew I had a duty to shield the patients from the presence of death, which would only become apparent when the body was slipped away on a trolley through the ill-lit ward, for the hour was well after midnight.

I contacted the night sister, aware that I had to keep my emotions well under control. Nurses do not cry. Her manner was brusque and businesslike. There was a body to remove from the ward. Slowly she inspected my charts; she could find no fault. I was questioned as to the manner of death, then instructed to lay out the body: to wash and reclothe John ready for his mother's visit. Sister later inspected my work. Her eyes slowly swept around the screens separating John from the rest of the ward, in which there were twenty-three patients. She twitched a curtain with her fingers. 'There is a gap here, nurse. Doubtless the other patients were made fully aware of all your proceedings. You must have both disturbed and upset them. Now I will have to make a report to matron. I will come again within the hour to inspect your work.'

It was her only criticism; but each word was like a whiplash. I knew that there had been no identifiable gap, and I had been well aware that patients needed both silence and privacy during the night hours. But I also knew that any protestations I made would only make the situation worse. This night sister would always find faults. In the meantime, my prime duty was to John and his mother. Gently I washed his body for the last time and put fresh linen on his bed while awaiting his mother's arrival, whereupon she sat closely by my side.

Together we wept; then she prayed, clutching the cross around her neck. Even today, I still muse upon the words Aslan the Lion said to the dead children on that final page of *The Last Battle*, the final book in C.S. Lewis's Narnia series: 'The term is over; the holidays have begun. The dream is ended: this is the morning.' In death, John was finally at peace; together his mother and I grieved.

Sensing his presence, her tears slowly subsided. His life, his adventures in the army, had only been the cover. He was beginning, as C.S. Lewis wrote, 'Chapter one of the great story, which no one on earth has ever read: which goes on forever: in which every chapter is better than the one before.' The memory of John and his mother will always remain with me.

During my time in that ward there were incidences when light lit up the darkness. Sam, a tall muscular African, was admitted dying of pneumonia. His life was dramatically saved with penicillin. The year was 1947. As penicillin had only been in use since 1939 it still seemed like a miracle drug. It was wonderful to see this man return to full life. I will never forget the day that his extended family arrived in the ward, sweeping past the indignant sister, in spite of her proclamations that only two visitors were permitted for each patient at one time. Sam's bed was surrounded with friends and family. Everyone burst into hymns of praise, with each visitor singing at his own pace. The children clapped their hands in joy, while a small baby, snuggling up to his mother's breast while feeding, smiled and burped in satisfaction. It was a picture never to be forgotten. A much-loved husband and father had been returned to his family, and they expressed their joy in song and laughter, and their Father God was praised.

Sally Anne was just eighteen years old and at the beginning of her university life when she was admitted with meningitis, once a fatal disease. The sulphonamide drugs had only been discovered in 1932, and fifteen years later were still not completely free from toxic effects. Sally survived, but became profoundly deaf. Her lifestyle had changed, yet I still remember the merry smile on her face, those red curls bobbing as she helped transport patients in wheelchairs along to the toilet. Then there was seventeen-year-old Herbert. He had grossly infected heart valves. Over a period of time, his life was sustained by massive doses of injected penicillin. He used to drink enormous quantities of lemonade, brought in by his solicitous relatives. He took inordinate pleasure in the fact that one penny would be given for the return of each empty bottle. Every week, on my free day, I would return those bottles to the little local shop, and reclaim the money for him. I can still picture his smile of thanks. Pennies were then of some importance to young people, and were still much valued in those days.

Grandma Hymphen was over eighty years of age. She was confined to bed. More than anything else she wanted a corset to compress her protuberant belly. No words of reasoning would dissuade her. She described in detail the type required, which seemed to me to be a style that was no longer in fashion, or even made any more. While off duty, I went to all the major department stores within Oxford Street in London, and was met with sympathetic smiles. I explored all the street's smaller shops, and then those in my home town. Week after week I came back on duty with the same story. There had been no success. This never deterred Grandma Hymphen. She died happily in her sleep, uplifted in the belief that I would go on searching, and that one day her corset would finally be found.

I often wondered about Jimmy. I got to know him in my second year of training, when I was working on a children's ear, nose and throat ward while on day duty. He was admitted from casualty with a history of 'having accidentally fallen downstairs, sustaining a fractured skull'. As a result, his hearing was affected in one ear. He seemed unduly frightened, and would stare up at me with large mournful ever-tearful eyes, his thumb permanently positioned in his mouth. At times, he rocked his body in a tortuous manner. Although five years old, Jimmy still wet his bed every night, and howled with grief when admonished by the senior nursing staff.

I grew very fond of Jimmy. I devised a tactic that went against all the teaching theories of the time to do with child development. I promised to give him a penny bar of Nestlé chocolate after breakfast each day, if he managed to keep his bed dry. I told him that I did this because I loved him more than anyone else in the ward, but that it had to be our very special secret. I also promised to wake him up in the night, so that he could empty his bladder. He happily learnt to use the urinal, also known as 'the bottle' by the male patients.

It worked. Soon Jimmy was waking up by himself, and asking me if he could use a bedpan. Jimmy remained dry until I was transferred from night duties to day. Breakfast had been served before I arrived on duty, and his bed was soaking wet. Jimmy looked up at me, with tears streaming down his cheeks. Slowly he stuttered: 'Nursie, my nursie, it don't matter, do it?'

I assured him that it didn't, as I remade his bed, and gave him a good wash, along with some fresh pyjamas. I told him that I still loved my Jimmy; however, that red-covered chocolate bar would come after breakfast whenever I was on day duty, and that it would have to remain a secret from Sister, otherwise there was a possibility that I might lose my nursing job in her ward.

Jimmy never wet his bed again, at least while he was in hospital. I have often thought about him over the years, remembering those black bruises around his face and upper body, along with those puzzling healed fracture lines seen on the X-rays of his rib cage when he was first admitted to hospital. I can't help thinking about his fears and uncertainties, and the fact that his parents never once came to visit. Later I wondered whether he had been a victim of child abuse. At the time, it seemed to me that most doctors tended to regard childhood injuries as accidental. It must have been intolerable, even for medical people, to contemplate parents behaving violently towards their own children, inflicting both physical and emotional damage. Jimmy, I often wondered whether you were filled with untold terrors on your return home. Yes, I often thought about you and wondered whether you managed to survive such sufferings during your years ahead of you.

There was also Rachel, a young nurse admitted from our casualty department, who had taken a massive overdose of aspirin during her off-duty period. I remember her despair and her tears. She nearly died. The young casualty doctor had not rested for ten hours when she first arrived. When she appeared in his ward, he was trying to find a suitable vein to give a blood transfusion to the drunken driver of a van that had crashed into a car, killing the mother, and seriously injuring both her two young children.

'You are wasting everyone's time,' he said angrily, after taking her clinical history. 'You, a nurse, you should have known better.'

Rachel never fully recovered from her self-hate, from her feelings of shame. She said very little to the questioning doctor; however, we became firm friends. She revealed her problems to me, but only after I had promised to keep her words secret. 'You must vow to be like a priest. Never ever betray me to anyone else.'

What else could I say or do? I gave her my solemn word and listened, and so she told me her life story. Rachel had been sexually abused by her father since her very early childhood. She had tried to escape her father's attentions by entering into nursing training; she thought she had escaped, until the illness of her mother necessitated her special leave to return home from hospital duties. Again Rachel was tormented: this she endured for the sake of her depressed mother. Finally, her father refused to allow her to return to hospital for the completion of her training. Rachel, feeling that her escape hatch of nurse training would be forever closed against her, had decided to end her miserable existence. In this she had failed. Rachel had been seized with despair. Her life was filled with darkness.

Dear friend Rachel; how you suffered. In a sense, such secrets were the privilege of nursing. Medically she was assumed fit after undergoing the misery of stomach washouts and intravenous infusions to restore the fluid and electrolyte balance in her body. I thought I had done my best. I bought goodies for her, and chatted to her in my off-duty times, for she never had any visitors. I naively assumed that somehow our friendship together would give that healing touch, that Rachel would return to the nursing she had grown to love. It was never to be: the scarring, the emotional injury was too great. She was discharged as physically fit, and returned to her father's house.

Rachel's next attempt at suicide was successful. Would it perhaps have helped if I had broken my word, had betrayed that solemn promise made between two special friends? Perhaps psychiatric help would have healed her body and mind. Perhaps we both were too frail to face such a challenge. I shall never know: I was left suffering from feelings of sadness and guilt.

Could Rachel's life have been saved following such a betrayal of friendship? Suicide was a subject never discussed during our nursing training within the preliminary training school. In retrospect, I think that it was a sad omission. It was a topic on which guidance was essential. Patients would sometimes prefer giving such confidential information to the attending nurse, rather than to the doctor who was in charge of their case. There was less shame talking to a nurse than a doctor with his white coat and stern expression.

Some of the serving ward sisters tried to act like a consultant in their treatment of the young trainees, believing themselves to be in sole charge of a situation. This was reflected by one particular sister under whom I served. Senior nurses were expected to sacrifice their free time when in charge of a seriously sick patient. Junior nurses were not expected to go off duty, even after their long night shift, until certain tasks had been carried out to Sister's entire satisfaction. Patients were woken at 6 a.m. sharp each morning. Each patient's breakfast had to be served by the one junior night nurse on duty, and also cleared away, even if she had also been given the extra duty of helping with an emergency admission. Each patient within the beds numbering one to three, those adjoining the ward entrance, had to receive a 'blanket bath' if unable to wash themselves. The same beds then had to be remade to the hospital's exacting standards.

Another sister under whom I served always placed the most helpless patients, each of whom were in need of personal attention including a blanket bath, within those three beds adjoining the ward entrance. There were always, in my training time, only two nurses serving on night duty, the junior, one of whose many tasks was to leave the sluice both clean and tidy, alongside the completion of those blanket baths, before she went off duty. On some occasions, the kindly senior nurse would help her junior complete her tasks, before the time that the day sister arrived on duty. During my training, I was blessed with such a staff nurse while working on night duty in a medical ward. It was both a joy and privilege to work along with Joan. She was always ready to give both advice and information. Joan was always my strong support while I was on duty. She not only cared for her patients, but also for her junior staff.

There was only one sister working in charge of all the wards during the night period. She had to be available if advice was necessary. Some of the young doctors would sway with weariness as they were called from their sleep to examine a patient admitted as an emergency during the night, and then the night nurses so often had to prolong their stay on the ward, culminating in the loss of their breakfast, which was only served within set hours and never saved for those arriving late off night duty. Life seemed to be so very hard at times. However, I always enjoyed my times with those patients. Some of those ward sisters were superb, and one felt privileged to work within their team of nurses. University College Hospital had a very fine reputation, not only among its patients, but also with those within its nurse training school.

I preferred working within a men's ward. For some odd reason, the men used to call me Jackie. I think someone must have thought my name was Jacqueline; however, the name stuck, and I liked it. The health-ier among those men seemed to take a positive joy in both cooking and serving breakfasts, which relieved me of a major task. On the morning of my first night duty within this very busy male surgical ward, I had managed to burn the patients' breakfast porridge. The men never complained. It had taken me quite a long time to serve the 'special diets', which came up from the hospital kitchen. Some patients also remained unwashed when the day sister arrived on duty. Her scowling face had not allowed me to go off duty and walk away from a dirty sluice. I had finally completed my duties an hour later, consequently missing breakfast and falling straight into bed. I was to learn that a competent nurse always had some food secreted within her locker, even though such hoarding was expressly forbidden, since the practice was considered unhygienic.

Following the misery of my first night duty, an ex-naval cook, a patient within the men's ward, had taken over the task of both the preparation and serving of all the breakfasts; perhaps even more important, these patients had succeeded in making me laugh at myself. It was the very best of medicine. Other patients declared themselves prepared to wash and shave their friends, and even announced that 'they liked making beds'. In spite of my protestations, those men always insisted upon their self-imposed tasks; all of those patient tasks were, of course, strictly forbidden. One of the older men, who had experienced many admissions over the years, always winked and smiled when he spoke to me; some of his words are remembered.

'Your day sister, that blonde job. I did it for her many a time: no hustle nurse. She is tough now; she would not want me to tell upon her now, would she? You are too soft … need to toughen up: you need protecting. We will look after you.'

Following those horrendous hours endured on my first night of service within that male ward, the place functioned like clockwork. Smiling faces, feet neatly tucked under meticulously cornered sheets, greeted the day sister each morning. The sluice shone: even she could find no fault. Those male patients of mine had performed their self-imposed duties to a very high standard, certainly higher than I had been able to achieve. Each and every patient capable of such help gave me a hand in the ward maintenance. It was a pleasure to work along with those men; in their ward, Jackie remained my name.

Many of my friends were certainly not so fortunate while serving on night duty during their training. I happened to be one of the lucky ones. I felt privileged to be under the care of those male patients; together we were the perfect team.

Each week the men ran their own football pool. Gambling was strictly forbidden by Matron, but those patients always managed to organise the event. One weekend, I was told that I had won. I had not even made a contribution, and being a strict Methodist at the time,

I obstinately refused to accept the proceeds of a gamble. Somehow those men managed to secrete the winnings, a new ten-pound note, into the inner lining of my nurse's cloak. It was certainly a lot of money in those days. Priggishly I informed them all that it was going to charity, yet still they continued with their many kindnesses towards me. I formed a special bond with an old man who had been severely burned, and needed regular injections of penicillin. Several years later, he saw me while I was walking along London's Oxford Street. I did not recognise him initially, but he ran across the road trying to catch up with me, shouting out again and again to the amusement of the passers-by:

'Jackie, Jackie, remember me? You used to give me those injections into my bum.'

Yes, those men were lovely patients.

It was not always quite the same in the women's wards. Worn out with their household chores, most were happy to have their breakfasts served while still within their beds. There seemed none of the jollity, none of the raucous laughter, and certainly none of the banter that was a feature of the men's wards. Many women, when discharged, returned home to household duties along with looking after aged or ailing parents, or young children: most of those ex-patients needed a holiday, yet such chores remained their welcome. I still remember Rosie. In early pregnancy, she had a developing speech disorder, noted by her astute family doctor. She was placed in a bed alongside that of a severely handicapped woman in her late forties, whose speech could barely be understood. Rosie overheard the medical students discussing the patient's disease in detail, and only then did she come to realise the implications of her own ongoing incurable condition, the causation of which was unknown, there apparently being no magical cure with medication.

'Am I really going to be like that?' she whispered to me. 'What about my husband, my poor baby? What is going to happen to me, and to them?'

Rosie had been married for just a year. I dared to ask Sister why she had been placed adjoining that particular patient. The answer was simple: both women were under the care of the same physician, a consultant neurologist.

Patients at that time were often not made aware of their diagnosis. One such lady, Gwen, had inoperable cancer of the ovary. We would talk together, and I knew she was longing to return home, although she felt no better. She was advised to go to a convalescent home for a short period; and so one of my favourite patients departed, anticipating a brief holiday. She wrote to me later, telling me that as the ambulance transported her to that home, she had seen a large sign arching above the gates of entry, reading 'HOME FOR THE INCURABLES'. I kept that sad letter for many a month. Gwen was devastated. She insisted upon her right to die within her home, with her beloved husband by her side.

Later, that sign was removed.

Chapter 3

Nursing procedures became more challenging as one became more senior. Two years passed by quickly, and I became the proud owner of a 'striped belt', denoting my seniority, in exchange for the lowly 'white belt' of the junior probationer. Naturally the responsibilities were greater: the final examinations for State Registration were in sight, the success of which would ensure the wearing of the honoured 'blue belt'. I did enjoy the stimulation of studying, and eagerly looked forward to becoming qualified: a State Registered Nurse or SRN.

I spent a period of time serving on the obstetric ward during my time of nurse training. There was a case that continued to sadden me. A young woman was admitted from the casualty department. Apparently she had been seen wandering around the streets late at night, clearly under the influence of alcohol. Elisabeth was reported to the police by a passer-by. The policeman who came to her side saw that she was in pain, and then came to the realisation that not only was she in the later months of pregnancy, but also she had suffered a knife wound to her upper arm. She was transported by ambulance to casualty, where her wound was cleansed and stitched up. Apparently the blood loss had not been excessive: the wound was apparently self-inflicted.

Elisabeth had been admitted to the obstetric ward on which I was serving; fortunately, my registrar happened to be on duty, which was a great relief. The patient was a teenager. It was clear that she was in the late stage of labour, and finally a baby boy was delivered. He was five pounds in weight, which was somewhat lower than the normal weight at birth. Initially the registrar had been quite concerned; however, the baby seemed determined to survive. Communication with Elisabeth was not easy. I did my best. Initially she would only tell me her Christian name; gently I insisted upon other details, and finally she told me her full story. She had been in a boarding school since early girlhood, having little contact with her parents who seemed to spend most of their time abroad on business. School holidays were often spent with an ageing aunt, during which time Elisabeth became very lonely. Secretly, and without her aunt's knowledge, during her early teens she became addicted to alcohol, bottles of which she had found in her aunt's home. As alcohol makes one lose one's inhibitions, she had allowed herself to become sexually promiscuous while attending some local youth clubs during the school holidays. Her parents remained absent, having apparently passed over total guardianship of their child to the father's older sister. Elisabeth always ate alone while living in her aunt's home, and her increasing girth remained unnoticed and she missed school in the later stages of pregnancy, while both parents remained abroad. It was a situation that I never understood, but had apparently been accepted both by her aged guardian and the school. However, I considered the final outcome to be quite remarkable.

Following the birth of the baby boy, it had amazed me when Elisabeth, following her rather difficult delivery, came to a decision to breast-feed. Initially I had anticipated a total rejection of her baby. The two bonded, and for the very first time, I saw Elisabeth's face wreathed in smiles while she fed her baby. She looked like a happy mother. I sat by her one afternoon during my off-duty time, while her baby, whom she had decided to call David, finally finished breast-feeding. Suddenly she had turned to me, her face lit with joy while she spoke: 'No one has ever loved me before. And now, for the first time in my life, I have someone to love. No one is ever going to take him away from me: just no one.'

It seemed to me that Elisabeth had come to the right decision. A distant relative of her father's visited unexpectedly one afternoon, along with his wife. The couple were relatively young, probably within a few years of approaching middle age. It was quite evident that my patient enjoyed their visit. Just before they left for home, Elisabeth put her beloved baby into the arms of the smiling wife. I had watched them all very carefully, wondering whether a problem was about to be solved. Surely not: for Elisabeth had vowed never to be parted from her baby. Surely she would never part with her newly born beloved son.

I pondered over those words she had said, while keeping my eyes upon her two visitors. Suddenly they rose, along with promises to come yet again. Following their departure, I hastened to the side of my patient. Her face was again wreathed in smiles. They had promised to take the baby into their home. She looked at my solemn face, clutched my hands, and chuckled while she spoke. The laugh was infectious, and I laughed along with her.

'I just do not understand,' I said at last. 'Why are you so happy? What has happened?'

'Michael and Moira want to take my baby into their home, and I have agreed.' Her eyes sparkled while she spoke, remaining fixed upon my face. There was a challenge in her tone of voice. It was a situation that puzzled me completely.

'You told me that you would never ever be parted from your David, that he was your son for life.'

'He is my son till the end of my life. I will love him for ever.'

'I just do not understand. Please explain.'

My words were followed by more laughter, and more smiles. Suddenly my young patient leant towards me, clutching my hands while she spoke.

'You see, they both explained ... they can never have any children of their own. Moira had a major operation two years ago. So they had both decided to adopt a baby. They are both longing to have a baby in their home. They both fell in love with David.'

'But ... but ...' I interrupted. 'You told me that you would never part with your David. You made a vow to me.'

'I won't tease you any longer. Michael and Moira want us *both* to come into their home, *David and me*. We seem to get on very well together, and Michael has got a very good job, so they can manage financially. He sometimes goes abroad, and Moira gets lonely, so she really needs company. They are both so keen to have a baby in the house, so we will both be made welcome. There is plenty of room for both of us, and then there will be no need for them to adopt a baby. Moira said it had always been her dream to have a newborn babe in her home. She was devastated when she was told by the surgeon after her operation that she could never have a child of her own.'

Elisabeth went on talking while David was still snuggling in her arms, burping contentedly. 'I asked about those parents of mine. Michael has been in touch with my father, I won't call him Dad; he has never been a dad to me. I have no real parents. Apparently he has decided to stay in Sweden until retirement, building up his business market. I guess he will stay there for life. He will be told about my situation, so there will be no problem. You know that he has a living-in housemistress, so his house here will be safe. I think it will be sold once they both decide to stay in Sweden. I hope they do, forever. I will not go back to college, never. I must look after my David. He is my son, yes, my son for life.'

Elisabeth had had no love from her parents; it was such a sad situation. However, it appeared that the problem had been solved. Elisabeth and her baby would be in safe hands. I remained certain that the final outcome would be happy for that new family. It seemed like a miracle to me. Elisabeth had been blessed, along with her beloved son, David. All would end well for both of them, of that I was convinced.

Nursing duties could be both wearisome and challenging at times. I think that the periods I really did not like so much were those of night duties. There were only two nurses serving by night, one senior and one junior. I never liked being on the ward alone then, left in sole charge, just in case an unfortunate incident occurred.

There was one occasion that I never will forget; it had happened while I was serving on night duty. I was told to 'special' a young woman to whom a blood transfusion was being administered. The kindly night sister informed me about the patient's condition, advising me to read her summary of the young woman's medical notes before commencing care. The patient had been an emergency admission, first seen in casualty, from where she had been directed to my ward.

The patient, whose name was Mary, was a college student. She had attended a student celebration party one weekend. Celebrations had lasted over the long hours of the night, and there had been alcohol available in abundance. Mary, drinking alongside her friends, had completely lost count of time, and finally had fallen asleep on the floor. On the following day, feeling nauseous, and struggling to open her eyes, she had found herself sleeping naked alongside two of the male students. She managed to force herself to her feet, but only felt fit enough to return to her own room later on in the day. She had been raped. It had been her very first sexual experience.

Mary was admitted to casualty in the early evening some three months later, being discovered in a near-unconscious state by a college friend who had called upon her, being concerned that she had failed to attend any of her lectures during that day. The two students lived in shared accommodation, and had been close friends during their college life together. Mary had come to the sudden realisation that she was in her third month of pregnancy. Her life had become a disaster.

Mary told me her story, flushing with shame as she spoke. I was sitting by her bed, questioning her gently, trying to give comfort. It was painful to listen to a young girl nearing nineteen years who had suffered such indignity. Mary had come from an unhappy family back-ground, but she had excelled in school, finally obtaining very high examination grades in her A levels. My patient suddenly clasped my hands as she talked. Her ambition as a girl had always been to become a hairdresser, much to her parents' anger, but it had always been her sole aim in life. Parental pressure had, however, won the day. Mary found herself forced into college; her father was an esteemed consultant physician, wanting his only child to achieve a similar status to his own. Mary finally acceded to his will and felt that she had been forced to follow in his footsteps; she didn't see any other alternative.

Mary's voice had trembled while she continued talking to me. When she discovered she was pregnant she decided to 'end it all', those being the exact words she used. She had swallowed a large quantity of aspirin tablets, which she had bought in divided doses from the two local chemists, thinking the end would be peaceful. Her college friend had found her in her bedroom, her face on the floor, surrounded by her own vomit. She was barely conscious. Mary told me that the stomach pains had been awful, there had been ringing noises in her ears, and she had been unable to see clearly. Stumbling, she had tried to locate her bed, all to no avail. Finally, feeling intensely nauseous, she had flopped, sprawling downwards upon the floor, all her muscles in spasm, and unable to move.

I felt intensely sorry for Mary. She thought that for her such an end would be easy, that the swallowing of pills would solve all her problems. Her life had been saved by her friend, along with the care we gave her in hospital. Initially she had felt no joy in continuing life. Unlike Rachel, the nurse who had been told by her consultant that 'she should know better', for Mary there had been help at hand.

The father of a college friend was a qualified counsellor, who arranged counselling while she was still in hospital. Once she had recovered physically from her ordeal, Mary was transferred to a gynaecological ward, where she had an abortion. It had been for Mary a mortifying experience.

I believe that nursing care is of vital importance to hospital patients, and involves the care of the body and the mind; great healing can be derived initially from the comforting presence of the attending nurse. Even the silent presence of another caring human being can work wonders. I witnessed many a nurse bring a smile, even a chuckle, to the face of an ailing patient.

Healing of the mind was of vital importance to Mary. I did my best while she was in the ward. Her parents didn't come to her visit her. Her only visitor was her college friend over the weekend, which was a blessing for Mary. Counselling on a regular basis was to continue after she had returned home. She had decided not to go back to college, which meant she had to give up her rooms. Where, I wondered, would she live? The answer came on the following Sunday, just prior to her discharge. I felt very surprised when Mary gave her college friend a prolonged hug during her visit. Later, Mary told me that she would be allowed to share the rented accommodation with her friend.

I was contacted on just one occasion following her discharge. Mary had taken a temporary post in a major supermarket; she was aiming to save some money, enough to allow her to achieve her ambition to train as a hairdresser. She continued to share her friend's rented accommodation, while still remaining separated from her parents. I often wondered whether Mary somehow managed to heal the rift between herself and her family at a later date. She had a hidden depth of determination, which I admired.

Chapter 4

Medical cases never failed to interest me. I enjoyed my times within the surgical, gynaecological and obstetric wards, but those disciplines did not have quite the same fascination as medicine. I longed to serve on a medical ward when finally qualified, the wards where diagnoses were made following various investigative procedures, drugs were prescribed to treat diseases, and the body became healed. There were always some illnesses for which a cure was not possible; nevertheless, drugs could ease a patient's suffering, and we tried to provide kindly care. There was always so much to learn, both by the doctor and the nurse, so much to achieve for each and every patient. Care of the patient, along with the possibility of a cure, was always the ultimate target for the medical staff.

I still remember one woman admitted late one evening into casualty following a fit in the street. She had been found by a member of the public, and an ambulance had been called. The patient seemed quite confused, and unable to give either her name or address. Eventually, after being examined by the casualty doctor on duty, she was transferred to the medical ward, on which I was serving. Initially a clear diagnosis had not been made. I was told to become the patient's 'special care' nurse. There was not thought to be a problem with alcoholism, and following a visit by the senior registrar, it was decided to take some blood to test. The patient became very angry when the houseman, a male doctor, attempted to take a blood sample, and she nearly succeeded in punching him in the face. She had to be restrained. Standing by her side, I attempted to soothe her while firmly grasping her hands. She was an older woman, and she seemed terrified of needles. It was something that I had generally observed among small children, and occasionally with teenagers.

Eventually the patient was identified by another woman in the ward. The patient was once the highly respected headmistress of a large state school. However, she became aggressive and bullying when dealing with colleagues and the pupils within her school. Still only in her early fifties, there had been widespread relief in the community following the head's enforced retirement. Later a national newspaper published some unpleasant details concerning both the physical and verbal abuse inflicted by the head-mistress upon some of the younger children.

It was discovered that the fits leading to her hospital care had followed a physical attack by some local youths late one night within the town centre. She had been rendered semiconscious; alerted by a passer-by, an ambulance had transported her to hospital. Fortunately she had a younger sister, a boarding school teacher, living in another distant location, who was enabled to take special leave, and stay at her sister's bedside. But she couldn't stay for long, and she didn't visit again. As her 'special nurse', I was advised to watch her closely, and record anything I thought might be indicative of early dementia, as she had remained semicon-scious on admission. I was also responsible for her care, which included making sure she ate her food. Alone, she tended to drop her food upon the floor. Eventually she learned to accept my help without too much disruption, and even gave the occasional smile. Patience was essential in dealing with this patient.

What the villagers had observed before her hospital admission was a gradual impairment in the headmistress's mental state. Neighbours noted that she seemed to have lost the ability to perform voluntary movements care-fully or express her thoughts clearly. Teachers within her school had initially noted the deterioration of her short-term memory. This led to aggressive behaviour, following which some of the children refused to attend school. Soon, her behavioural problems were reported to the local police by staff serving in the local shops. She had become really disruptive, and the most unwelcome customer of all time.

Like her villagers, I too observed this aggressive pattern of behaviour while acting as her 'special nurse'. It had frightened me at times. Apparently the woman had always vigorously denied that she had any problems when offered help and advice by her neighbours; she had also firmly refused to visit her family doctor.

It was only while in hospital on our ward that the patient was finally diagnosed as suffering from Alzheimer's disease, an illness affecting the brain tissue, causing dementia. The condition, named after the German neurologist Alois Alzheimer, affects both middle-aged and elderly people. It later transpired that a similar problem had been diagnosed with a relative, who had died while in a rest home some several years earlier. The patient was eventually discharged from hospital. It was decided that she was not able to care for herself, and she was placed in suitable accommodation to be cared for,

for the rest of her life. At that time, there was no known treatment for the disease.

The ward sister seemed unsure of her patient's final prognosis, but it did not appear to be good. I thought it to be such an incredibly sad situation for the patient. Initially the school had flourished under her leadership as headmistress. She had a first-class academic record, and was once highly respected in her local community. Had there truly been really no family love that could soothe her spirits? Did she really have to both live and die alone in the world? After that first visit, even her sister failed to stay by her side. While she would be looked after in a home, I believed that the loving concern of both friend and family, alongside physical contact with the sick patient, remained absolutely vital for healing both the body and the mind. In the presence of loved ones, both during the times of daily living, and also during the act of dying, a patient can find peace of mind: that is my belief. Some sixty years onwards, Alzheimer's disease is still under ongoing research within the medical world.

I will always remember the times when I used to return to my parents' home while on leave from my nursing service. It was a really relaxing and enjoyable time away from some of those troubled experiences while on my nursing duties within the ward. I was spoilt at home, sitting in the garden when the sunshine permitted, my head buried in my favourite books; A.J. Cronin remained one of my most-read authors. Sometimes my mother and I would visit a local cinema. Going back to the church of my childhood was also a time of joy.

Nursing had truly opened doors for me. I loved to listen to patients telling me about the important events in their lives. It helped me look back upon my own life in childhood fondly, remembering one of my English lessons while still at school. A short story competition had been set up by our English teacher. We had two weeks to write it. Never will I forget that teacher standing in front of her class waiting to give the name of the winner. Unsmiling, her head erect, she faced her class, and my name was announced. Overcome with joy, I gave her a grin, gripping the sides of my desk to stop myself rising to my feet. I finally raised both my arms in joy, turning my smiling face to all my friends. For a short period in time, our teacher remained unsmiling. Taking a step towards her pupils, and clasping her hands, she had announced in a rather strident voice, fixing her eyes firmly upon my face: 'There are, however, *sixteen* spelling mistakes.' Only then did she smile.

I would always use that memory to raise my spirits, to make me smile during those times when I felt utterly exhausted or when a particular night sister's comments had seemed too critical. My spelling did improve in the years ahead.

I always met up with the other probationer nurses for our evening meal while we were on night duty. There at the dining table, we restored our spirits with a good chat and made plans for a social time together on the next day when we weren't working, and after we had had some much-needed sleep. Some of the probationers, and that included me, never found it easy to sleep during the daytime. I always longed to return to day duties within the hospital wards, as did most of my friends.

I will never forget one patient whom I cared for in our surgical ward. She had been admitted following a fall in the local park while exercising her small dog. Sylvia had fractured her femur, the large bone in the upper part of the leg. Somehow she had managed to fall against a low-lying branch that projected out from the trunk of an aged oak tree while chasing her dog during play. I had spent some of my off-duty period with the patient when, following her request, she was surrounded with screens. The kindly ward sister had permitted privacy.

Sylvia begged me to weave her words into a story. While a hospital patient, she had read a women's magazine, and this had made her want to write a story based on one of the most important days in her life. Sylvia explained that she had always found it difficult to express herself in writing, and the story she had attempted to write had never been accepted for publication.

Sylvia, I learnt a lot about nursing care while you were a patient of mine. An understanding of a patient's background only comes from listening, and I learnt so much about you while you talked to me about your daughter. Sylvia, I have done my best for you. Yes, I have written your story. Yes, it was finally published.

I was off duty when Sylvia told me her story. She had been discharged from hospital that very morning. We happened to meet again while ambling around Regent's Park, and there she again talked to me about her life. We sat down together.

Initially Sylvia had sat silently by my side, her blue eyes remaining fixed upon my face. The early morning sun glinted gently on her hair hanging loosely over her hunched shoulders, highlighting the silvery streaks that fringed her broad forehead. Clearly visible were the fine wrinkles set in the smoothness of her skin. Suddenly the fullness of her soft lips had mouthed a whisper.

'I'm taking you back in time to that one special day. It all happened some four years ago. Write my story as though you were by my side, watching me, my invisible witness. Write how you would have seen me at that time, please, you are my only friend. I will tell you exactly how I felt on that special day. You must translate all my words into the story that I should have written; the story that should have been published.' Sylvia sat and watched me pick up a pen and paper while she finished talking.

A short silence followed, then Sylvia continued. 'I still remember those first words I muttered when I woke up on that day I'll never forget: "Today I'm thirty-six years old, and I just know I look more like sixty. I might as well be dead. Nobody wants me. There is no point in living, no point at all." Those were my exact words.'

Sylvia had watched the tears oozing slowly down her pallid cheeks, as she gazed in a mirror drawn from her handbag. I sat quietly by her side, eyes fixed upon her face, listening to her words, translating them into a story as I wrote.

'Why,' she had wondered, 'does the sun still shine as it had shone on Sandra's birthday, two years back to the very day?' Sandra was her only child, who, on her fourteenth birthday, had suddenly left home, never to return. Alone, Sylvia had borne her loss, coming just one year following the death of her beloved husband Gareth, the father adored by her only daughter. I listened, pen in hand, fully concentrating upon her words, my eyes fixed firmly upon her face.

Early in the morning, Sandra had left home following a heated argument with her mother; she had promised to return in time for her birthday party later in the evening. But she had never returned. The police search for Sylvia's daughter resurfaced tortuously in her mind. It seemed she had disappeared from the face of the earth. Sandra, with her long golden hair, she who had been so like her father, even to the sparkling beauty of his blue eyes and his sudden mood swings. The two had been so close.

The sun still shone on Sylvia's face as she had turned sadly through the sliding French doors of her dining room. They overlooked a park, used by children as a play area. Once the room had been her daughter's favourite domain, a place echoing with happy shouts and girlish giggles along with her father's banter. In the distance,

Sylvia could see someone playing hide and seek along with a small girl. The woman was partially hidden under a willow tree. The little girl was shrieking with laughter, her golden curls bobbing over her shoulders as she romped around searching for her mother. Sylvia remembered those past days. Sandra as a small child, chasing her beloved father, laughter filling the air. Resolutely Sylvia turned her back upon the scene. Two long years had passed her by: would her daughter ever return?

'Please God,' she had whispered, 'let there be a miracle.'

Once she had believed in miracles, surrounded as she was with Gareth's love, overcome with joy when baby Sandra had been born. The persistent ringing of the front door bell broke into the blackness of her thoughts. Hastily drying her tear-streaked cheeks, she went to answer the door. She had, of course, forgotten: it was time for the second postal delivery. Her friendly postman was always so patient. He stood there, at the front door, smiling as always, holding a large envelope in his hands.

'Couldn't push *this* through your post box. That's all you have today. See you soon.'

Silently Sylvia had taken the envelope, clutching it to her chest, turning to gaze out through the French doors at the park yet again. Why, she wondered, did the little girl run towards her home, clap her hands, twisting and turning on her toes as she did so, her face wreathed in smiles. It could have been her daughter as a small child; the likeness was incredible. Was she having a nightmare? Again Sylvia's eyes scanned the scene. Suddenly the little girl, perhaps responding her mother's call, disappeared. Sylvia stayed by the French doors. Feeling saddened, her fingers trembling, she withdrew a large photograph from the envelope. A strangely familiar face stared back at her. Curly golden hair tumbled down to the shoulders of a small girl; deep blue eyes surrounded by long lashes gazed into her own. It looked like it could be a photograph of her daughter Sandra as a small child, yet it could not be, for surely the face was more oval in shape, and the cheekbones too high? Sylvia turned to her husband's portrait. Did his lips suddenly tremble in a smile? Did his thoughts direct her to think lovingly upon their daughter? How she longed for Gareth and Sandra to be by her side yet again, the three of them reunited.

Suddenly deep within her mind, she felt the birth of hope, the lifting of those dark clouds of depression that had shadowed her over the times since her daughter's disappearance. The photograph was a mystery. She gazed at it intently, her fingers trembling while she clutched it in her hands. Who had sent it, and why? The answer, she felt, would surely come. Closing her eyes, she shut out the scene, hearing only the twittering of birds as they flew among trees.

Still the sun shone hotly. Struck with an overwhelming sense of loneliness, Sylvia sank trembling into a chair. Suddenly the persistent ringing of her front door bell startled her. Still clutching the photograph between her fingers, she hurried to answer the door.

'Nanna, Nanna, it's me! Nanna.'

It was the little girl she had seen in the park. Behind her stood a young woman. Anxious blue eyes stared out from a thin pale face, and a mane of golden hair straggled over lean shoulders. Her clothes, unlike those of the child, were bedraggled. Sandra's hair had been gold. Was it all a nightmare? Small arms entwined themselves around Sylvia's waist. Gleeful eyes looked up into her own.

'Nanna, Nanna, I love you, Nanna.'

Sylvia knelt, clasping her in her arms. The child screeched in delight, tugging at her waist.

'Mother, it's me, Sandra.' The young woman's voice was slow and beseeching.

Trembling, Sylvia clasped her daughter's hands, leading her slowly to the dining room. Following her disappearance, she had prepared for her return every day. Even the flowers had been freshly picked from her garden on that very morning. A large chocolate-coloured teddy bear dominated the settee, cradling a smaller version of itself. The little girl leapt into the lap of the larger bear uttering cries of delight. Almost as if moved by an unseen force, Sylvia held out her arms, clasping the frail form of her daughter to the warmth of her body, smiling up into her beloved Gareth's portrait as she did so, her eyes fixed upon his face.

'I could see you through the window. We would have left if you hadn't kept looking at our photograph. I thought you might never want to see me again, not after I disappeared. I thought you might tear it up into little bits. You kept looking at it, and smiling,' her daughter whispered.

'Tell me, tell me what happened. Please tell me why you disappeared.' Sylvia was trembling with joy as she spoke.

'Dad and I were so close, and when he died I felt I couldn't bear to live without him. Somehow I got led into taking some drugs, so easy to get hold of, even at school. You didn't seem to notice, even when I took some of your money to pay for them. You never seemed to notice anything, not even when I got myself pregnant.

I had too much drink at one of our late-night parties. I couldn't bear it all, so I decided to do myself in, to run far away from you so I could never be found. You thought I was dead, didn't you? Well, I was in a way, only the baby kept growing inside me, and you had never noticed. You always looked so thin and frail. I dyed my hair red, only you never seemed bothered. I just wanted to die, to die alone. I didn't know where to go, so I just wandered the streets. One really stormy night, I found myself sleeping inside a village church. It was always open, so I stayed there by night, all by myself.'

Sylvia's arms gently tightened their grip around her daughter's waist as she talked. The little girl's eyes had closed in sleep, her head resting between the arms of the chocolate-coloured bear.

'It was there on one rainy night that I knew the baby was coming. There was a light glowing at the altar, and because it was so warm in the church, I thought it would be a safe place to leave the baby. Only then did I notice that I was not alone. There was a lady with grey hair kneeling; her hands were clasped together, and her eyes constantly closed in prayer. The pains got worse. I let out a cry and then some screams. I felt so scared, I knew the baby was coming. It terrified me. I screamed again.

Suddenly I felt the baby forcing its way out of me, and I let out even more screams, I was so frightened. I was just in front of the altar. Soon that lady came up to me and helped me. After it was over, she wrapped my baby up in her petticoat, and shielded me in her cloak. She took me to her home, she had a little car waiting outside. Yes, she took both of us. Mum, she promised to be like a priest and never tell anyone. She said she would always care for me and made me swear never ever to take drugs and drink again, not ever. She told me to call her Sara.'

'So just why did you leave her?' Sylvia interrupted gently.

'She had cancer, and before she died, Sara made me promise to come to you again and that is why she had our photograph taken. She made me promise to post it to you, telling me that it would show that I still loved you. She didn't have much money, but she gave me all she had; it meant that I could pay the fare home. You see, we had moved to Wales.'

'Gareth's country, his place of birth,' Sylvia whispered softly.

'Mum, I want to live with you again. Please, please.'

Two pairs of eyes turned to the sofa, where a small body was curled around the chocolate-coloured teddy bear.

'I called her Dorothy. Her name means "a gift of God", did you know that? You sat for such a long time staring through those windows. We played in front of you, and you didn't seem to notice. I thought about the photograph I had posted, and luckily it reached you today. We saw you staring at it. Our Dorothy looks like both of us, doesn't she? Mum, please forgive me. You must have thought that you would never ever see me again, that I was dead. For me, it seemed like a journey into hell, but now I have come back again.'

There was a short silence while they both looked up at Gareth's portrait. His smile was tender; his eyes seemed fixed upon the sleeping child. Sylvia felt his love embracing the family. She knelt down, and hugged the child. The little girl stirred in her sleep, then opened her eyes, whispering: 'Nanna, I love you. I love my Nanna. Please can we live here with you?'

'Stay with me. You must both stay with me, here in our home together.'

Turning towards her daughter, Sylvia's arms tightened around Dorothy while she spoke. 'Every day I got everything ready for you ... just in case you returned: even the flowers are fresh today; red roses of love taken from our garden.'

The rays of the noon day sun suddenly gleamed brightly on their faces. Sandra's voice spoke softly into her mother's ear. 'Mum, I'm sorry, so very sorry. Please forgive me.'

Sylvia embraced her daughter and grandchild. She smiled happily as she spoke. 'I love you both, you are my family. Let's go out to the park and play for a little while then afterwards I will take you both out for a meal. Together we will celebrate. It is your birthday today, and now we are all together again. I have been praying for a miracle, and now it has come. Let's go out now. We can start our celebrations by having an ice cream together.'

Lowering her head, Sylvia heard her daughter whispering softly: 'When I close my eyes, I can see my father smiling in heaven. He keeps on saying, "Thank you God, thank you for ever. Thank you for my family."'

Sylvia turned to me and smiled. She had finished telling me her story.

I always loved to listen to my patients' stories. Certainly, while still in hospital, Sylvia had told me that she had felt very low in spirit following her husband's death and that it was the one point in her life when she had contemplated suicide; she had made me promise never to divulge that to anyone, most especially to the medical staff. Undoubtedly she had entered a new life since Sandra's return, a life of happiness and peace of mind; of daily delight alongside her daughter and the gift of her little grandchild. A couple of years later, Sandra fell in love with a handsome young Australian, and they married. When they returned to Sydney, mother, daughter and grandchild had a tearful parting, but Sylvia this time knew where her daughter was, and the letters and postcards she received showed that they were happy. That was all she ever wanted for her child.

In fact, not long after our meeting together in Regent's Park, Sylvia had emigrated to Australia, there to live along with her daughter and grandchild.

I thoroughly enjoyed nursing at this point in time. I was quite happy attending to the patients' personal and medical needs. Life within the hospital was good, and I had made many friends among the nurses in training. Eileen was one in particular. Both her parents lived in Wales, so when a weekend together was available, it was spent at my home, and my friend came along with me and my family on our outings together. This helped to soothe her loneliness, for she felt far from her beloved Welsh home, far from those she loved.

Studies remained stimulating, and while travelling ahead in the road of nursing, there was always my vision of qualification: that of becoming a State Registered Nurse. However, there always remained an inner feeling of restlessness, of something not quite achieved. This puzzled me. Had I not set my sights on becoming a trained midwife, followed by missionary service in China? Why was I still not satisfied? It all seemed rather strange. A holiday became due, and I decided to put all these matters aside, and force myself to enter another world outside my hospital life. I was due to join some rambling friends in Cornwall, and there the matter could rest while my body and mind were refreshed. My nursing duties, and my involvement with patients, had absorbed all my attention. I needed a break.

Chapter 5

On my return back to my nursing duties, feeling thoroughly refreshed, I was asked to chaperone some medical students from other teaching hospitals. They were taking their practical examinations for their final qualification in medicine. I was absolutely fascinated. The patients all had interesting medical histories, and in turn each spoke of their problems and symptoms to the students. All patients exhibited physical signs on being examined, which were in most cases classical textbook descriptions of their disease. They had of course been selected very carefully by the consultants. I listened intently. It seemed to me that although I had been taught how to nurse patients, I had not always understood just why I was undertaking certain tasks. Watching those students made me feel envious; suddenly I had become somewhat dissatisfied with my current lot in life. Surely some sort of change was due. Somehow I felt challenged; and my spirits were strangely uplifted. It felt quite odd.

Many of the males seemed very sure of themselves; however, the only female candidate appeared to be very nervous. Female medical students were rare at that point in time. I felt sorry for this one, and the examiner seemed oddly abrupt with the young woman. I wondered if the reason was simply because of her sex; sometimes it seemed as if female students were resented by some of the consultants. One of the patients being examined, an elderly gentleman, who looked anaemic, purposely omitted to tell this female candidate that on occasions he was passing blood from his anus. Old-fashioned and courteous, he clearly felt that it was not an acceptable topic of conversation to have with a woman. Standing there, feeling sorry for the female medical student, I recalled a time when I was acting as a chaperone on a grand ward round with a nationally known consultant surgeon. He had made a very firm announcement to the students gathered round him: 'If you don't put your finger up it, then you will put your foot in it.'

Silently, I handed the woman a rubber glove. She opened her mouth to protest, but I looked her straight in the eyes, nodding as I did so. I had thrown down the gauntlet and the medical student had picked it up. The patient was horrified to be subjected to such indignity by a female, although he had always enjoyed a joke while being examined by male students. He protested loudly, but sister sternly rebuked him, and his anger suddenly subsided. Nevertheless, that procedure ensured that the correct diagnosis was presented to the examiner by the female candidate. Perhaps those practical examinations were not always absolutely fair, and nervous aspiring female doctors were sometimes bullied. I knew that I had exceeded my duties, but felt that under those particular circumstances, it was a reasonable and fair procedure.

Medicine continued to fascinate me. I was always happy to offer myself as a chaperone to male medical students as it gave me yet another opportunity to expand my knowledge.

In my final third year of training, I was placed in the private wing of my hospital (termed the Private Patients' Wing or PPW). At first, I missed being part of a ward team and the companionship I felt with many of my colleagues and ward patients. I viewed with apprehension the thought of being allocated just three patients, each in their separate private room. However, I soon enjoyed the time spent with each of them. They warmed to me and told me some fascinating stories. Some of these paying patients were famous. One I remember with sadness, for she died, was a celebrated singer with a wonderful soprano singing voice. I soon found it a privilege to be permitted to get to know them on a much more personal basis than was possible in the ward situation; there was more time to talk together with my patient within the privacy of his or her private room. I was also able to listen to each individual's anxieties about their health. I could, if necessary, always obtain advice for them. One of my private patients was the wife of the senior consultant in obstetrics and gynaecology working within University College Hospital. Instead of the usual box of chocolates as a leaving gift to me, she wanted to buy me 'something special'. A book token was suggested by the patient.

We had really enjoyed the time we spent talking together, and eventually I came to tell her my dream of some day training in medicine. It was something that I had never discussed with anyone else, apart from my mother, since the beginning of my nursing training. She listened intently. Later, just before her hospital discharge, she presented me with a marvellous medical textbook entitled *French's Index of Differential Diagnosis*. She had obviously consulted her husband about the best book to buy me. It became a much-treasured source of help and inspiration over the years ahead.

I obtained a first class in my final nursing examinations, along with the State Registration in Nursing, so I was able to proudly wear that prized 'blue belt' worn by a staff nurse. I treasure to this day the little badge awarded by the General Nursing Council, dated July 1949, that was an acknowledgement of my qualification. At the time, it was an unspoken agreement that all qualified nurses would stay on for a fourth year, not only to gain more experience, but also to serve the hospital responsible for their training. Originally, I had been happy with the prospect. However, I knew that some of my friends had planned to leave in order to get married, while others had made the decision to apply for a nursing post nearer to their home.

And now, I had fully set my heart on becoming a medical student. I learnt that grants had of late been made available to female medical students. I wondered: could my dream become a reality? But I had concerns. I realised that I would have to be dependent upon my parents for some financial support. I also felt lonely. I had many friends who were leaving to get married, and

I was longing for a partner in life: someone with whom I could share my thoughts; someone with whom I could later raise a family. This was another dream, along with a qualification in medicine.

My mother, who was always prepared to listen to me and discuss any problems, became quite alarmed, advising me keep my aspirations entirely fixed upon training in medicine. I never discussed marriage with my father; however, I knew that he had always wanted his daughter to turn to training of a more academic nature, one more prestigious, in his eyes, than nursing. I knew he would want to support me should I succeed in obtaining a college entry for a training in medicine.

I never thought of myself as a clever person, just determined and hard-working. I gave the matter a lot of thought. Perhaps after all, I was being over-ambitious, even foolish, to consider becoming qualified in medicine. My matriculation results had been good, but certainly not outstanding. My thoughts often became negative. Even if qualified in medicine, would a job be available for a female doctor? Perhaps it would be wise to continue with my nursing duties within University College Hospital, to become a ward sister before commencing midwifery training. I spent many hours thinking about where my future should lie, but somehow I failed to come to any firm decision.

The struggle within my mind was resolved for me in an unexpected fashion. Pondering moodily upon my dilemma one spring day while walking down a long avenue of trees laden with the beauty of green leaves, I became aware of the sudden chirruping of birds. Looking around me, I noticed for the first time the beauty of the buds bursting into blossom, the glory of the sun glinting gold upon the rough roundness of the tree trunks. On one of the lower branches was a mother bird, patiently enticing her reluctant youngster to fly. Slowly, painstakingly, the young bird hesitantly followed her, until at last he reached the topmost twig, alongside that of his mother. There, beside her, the small bird sang sweetly. He had faced his mother's challenge successfully. Entranced, I watched and listened. Finally both birds spread their wings, soaring through the branches, ever upwards out of my sight.

I felt that God had given me a message. I too had to look ever upwards, trustfully spreading my wings. I too would be guided in the journey through that tangled maze that was my tree of life, and in that struggle, I would never be left alone.

Chapter 6

I had now finally come to the decision to apply for a place to train in medicine in one of London's teaching hospitals. In great hope, I sent a letter to each, giving particulars of my nursing background. I decided not to approach University College Hospital, reasoning that a fresh start in another hospital would be best for me. I think I had deep concerns regarding my reference from the UCH Matron. She was in a position to talk with each of the consultants working within UCH, which would be a major disadvantage; I could not count on her support. Trained under the guidance of her hospital, I now failed to render any further service, having been awarded the SRN.

In that final interview, Matron, clothed in blue, had been an austere and forbidding personality. How majestically she gazed down upon me, her head held high behind her desk, a queen set upon her throne. The

silence stretched itself between us: I had to force myself
to speak, looking upwards into her face.

'Matron. I would like to give you notice. I need to
leave your nursing service because—'

Scythe-like, she cut through my hesitant words. 'You
want to leave now that my hospital has managed to instil
into you the requisite skills of nursing, and enable you
to become a state registered nurse?' There was a pause
as her lips tightened, and her forehead became furrowed
with a frown. 'I suppose you want to get married,' she
said acerbically.

'No, Matron, not married, not yet. I want to go
to medical college, and train as a doctor. Please could
you act as my referee?' I knew that I had to make this
request; there was for me absolutely no alternative. I had
no choice in the matter.

My voice was full of hope, and great expectations.
Surely she would help me? I had a legitimate reason for
wishing to leave nursing: I wanted to undergo further
exploration into that fascinating world of medicine.
Surely that could not be denied. Undoubtedly it was my
nursing experiences that had led into the field of medicine. The silence that followed lasted a full minute. Yes,
a few of my friends were leaving to get married, another

was pregnant, but when I looked at the deepening lines upon her forehead, I realised that to her my decision to study medicine was an even greater sin.

At last Matron spoke, a derisory smile stretching her lips. 'You really think that *you* could manage all that academic work along with all those long years of study?' Her nostrils quivered disdainfully as her finger flicked through a file. 'Your work here has by no means been exemplary. Indeed, it has been most unsatisfactory at times. There have been several unfortunate incidences certainly not conducive to the patient's welfare.'

Yes, there had been a few times when my behaviour had not been exemplary. The time when the dreaded blonde night sister had found me tightly clutched within the arms of a drunken patient admitted from the casualty department after he had crashed his motorcycle. It was the one occasion when I had welcomed her presence, for by her sheer authority, and amazing force, she had somehow managed to release me. Nevertheless, the blame had been laid entirely upon my shoulders. There had been another unforgettable event, when I cried in grief along with the shocked parents, following the unexpected death of their newborn baby son. It was perhaps the most abhorrent of sins: becoming emotionally involved with a patient. Undoubtedly my nursing career had been truly compromised by such incidents.

'Certainly you must use me as your referee. There is for you no other choice.' She gazed at me with clinical coldness; under her gaze I was a butterfly pinned down in captivity, and she dismissed me from her presence.

The replies from the various London teaching hospitals that I had applied to eventually arrived through the post. They had all rejected me, but I was waiting to hear from one more: St Bartholomew's hospital. I wondered: could there possibly be one last chance? I waited for that final reply to all those applications. Was there perhaps still an inborn prejudice against the input of female doctors into that honoured profession? It was then that my spirits became very low. Were my dreams about to be shattered? Had I made the decision to leave nursing at too early a stage in my career? Perhaps I should have carried on at University College Hospital for at least another year. Perhaps Matron had been right. My spirits became even more low while I waited for that final letter … surely it had to be one of rejection.

The year was 1949. I was nearly twenty-two years of age. I finally had a letter from the oldest teaching hospital in London, St Bartholomew's, informing me that I had been allocated an interview. It seemed unbelievable. I could barely believe my good fortune. I read and reread the letter. Was my dream about to become reality? Was I really going to be given the opportunity to study medicine within that male-dominated profession when so often it had seemed like an impossible ambition?

I decided to maintain my courage and convince myself that there had to be some chance of acceptance, however remote. I had to force myself to attend that interview allied with the determination to present myself as a competent and worthy candidate.

St Bartholomew's Hospital had been founded in 1123, and had a continuous history of patient care since that time. It seemed extremely important for me to select exactly the right ensemble for that red-letter day. My budget was limited: finally I stood in front of the mirror, and gazed long and earnestly at myself. I wore a rust-coloured suit devoid of feminine frippery, fashionably long-skirted, along with a white blouse and neat cravat. My blue eyes sparkled and my brown hair curled itself tightly under a minute bowler hat. I was devoid of make-up, and surely looked eminently professional. My parents certainly approved of their daughter's new image.

On the day of the interview at St Bartholomew's Hospital, I was directed down a long corridor studded with offices. I finally reached the seating area outside the dean's office. I was nervous, but I was also full of hope. I was, after all, a dedicated woman with three years of nursing experience behind me, and a qualified state registered nurse. I knew that Matron had received good references from the ward sisters under whom I had served, especially the one of German extraction; she really had been such a wonderful tutor. I still remember her fascinating ward rounds along with her student nurses; tutoring was one of her strongest points; she had been truly inspiring.

I was met outside the dean's office by a sea of expectant faces; some seemed to be competing for the attention of a very pretty candidate with a short flared skirt and flowered blouse. The only other female was dressed in a dark suit, and seemed to me to be in her late twenties. Looking grimly learned, she introduced herself as a first-class honours science graduate. Her references, she assured me, were impeccable. A muscular male from Wales seated himself beside me. I managed to extract from him how well he had done in his A levels and he also told me that he had applied to Cambridge University for the preclinical studies of anatomy, physiology and biochemistry. My heart began to sink. Faced with these candidates, had I even the remotest chance of success? I had no such first-class academic achievements, and had never had any ambition to attend a university.

Each applicant was finally called into the dean's office for their interview. At last came my turn. From behind an imposing desk, five men stared down upon me: as well as the dean, there was a physician, an obstetrician, a senior lecturer and a surgeon. I held myself upright while their eyes bored into mine. There was an initial silence after the dean had made the introductions. His eyes flickered from my tensely held form to Matron's long reference letter set before him. His voice seemed devoid of expression as he spoke.

'You have just completed your state registration in nursing, and have not chosen to repay your hospital by rendering service in the capacity of a staff nurse for just another year. This was an expectation of which you were well aware. Your hospital enabled you to gain the state registration in nursing; surely that service must be repaid.'

My tone was defensive. 'I have always wanted to train in medicine. My nursing service has taught me how to care for sick people; I am now very anxious to start my new training as soon as possible. I really do want to learn just how to diagnose my patients' illnesses and learn how to deal with their problems. I have recently been informed that women can now apply for a grant.'

'A grant ...' the physician said. The tone of his voice certainly sounded derogatory.

I thought upon the other candidates, how they exuded affluence and the advantages that a privileged education brings, all except for that Welshman, the one who had sat beside me while awaiting his interview. It seemed that he had not been born with a silver spoon in his mouth.

'There were, we are told, some noted difficulties that you experienced within your nursing training. Academically medicine requires long hard study; the dedication of a studious lifestyle.' Again it was the physician who spoke. There was a frown upon his face.

'I obtained a first class in both my written and practical hospital examinations.' I spoke with some spirit. Surely, I thought, those results must be of some value.

The elderly surgeon smiled sardonically. 'Yes, a first class in your nursing examinations. I suppose they gave them away with a cup of tea.'

They were his precise words, which I have never forgotten. His style of speech was so scornful. Evidently he had already made up his mind. There is a phrase that

I was to learn at a later time; it seems quite apt to apply it on this particular occasion: 'You can always tell a Barts' man, but you can't tell him much.'

I explained that only five nurses within my set obtained similar results to mine. However, my words seemed to be of no worth. Rejection was surely staring me in the face. Lips tightly pursed, the surgeon continued to face me, his eyes fixated firmly upon mine.

'If selected, you would of course take residence within our medical college.'

Those words, coming from that stern-faced surgeon, were a statement of fact; there appeared to be no choice in the matter: once selected, I had to conform.

'No, I could not afford to do so. I would live at home; the distance is not far.'

'I see, unfortunately travelling time is undoubtedly time wasted. Tell us about your hobbies.'

'I enjoy reading, writing short stories and I have just started writing a novel.'

'Stories, for women's magazines of course.' The scornful comment came from the senior college lecturer.

There was no time to answer. Another pair of eyes looked into mine, those of the obstetrician. In front of me was yet another frowning face.

'Biologically women are designed to procreate; raise a family. Medical students must remain dedicated. There is no time at all for diversions.'

'I am not going to get married, not at the moment. My aim is to become qualified in medicine. My life will be devoted to my studies.'

'You would want to take postgraduate training, become a consultant?'

'I want to become a family doctor.' I had already decided against telling them that I once had thoughts about becoming a missionary in China. In any case, service as a family doctor even for a relatively short period would undoubtedly provide a sound training service. I had not really reached a final decision.

'A family doctor, I see… That will be all.' Those were the obstetrician's last dismissive words, said with some scorn.

'Thank you. You may leave now; you will hear from me at a later date.' The dean smiled at me as he said those final words. His was the only smile. The interview was at an end. There were no more questions to be raised. Heads were lowered while I raised myself to my feet. There was no further interest in my application. Surely I had been rejected.

I gave them all a final despairing glance as I turned my back upon them, and left the office. I made my way rapidly through the huddle of the remaining candidates, ignoring the Welshman's enquiring eyes, and made my way into the anonymity of the hospital grounds. There, miserable, I mused while sitting upon a wooden bench, watching the sun sparkle upon the smooth surface of the fishpond. Several patients with some plaster casts passed by me, others were in wheelchairs, all being transported under the care of nurses and students. My heart sank. Never would I join them at Barts. Exhausted, I drifted into the depths of a despairing sleep. My cheeks were still wet with tears when I awoke some time later. I was alone. My dreams had been shattered, and I knew that for me there was no hope. Surely I had been rejected, there must be no other answer. My head was bowed, while my body became warmed by the gentle heat from the rays of sun that slowly emerged between the greyness of the clouds.

Suddenly I was conscious of a shadow. I had been cut off from the sun's rays by the body of a man towering over me. A familiar face with those peering brown eyes looked down upon me. It was the dean. 'I am glad to have found you. I am now on my way to lunch.'

I looked at my watch; two long hours had elapsed since my interview.

'I am one of the old school, and believe that a woman's place is within the home. However, I will not abide domineering females, in particular those who are matrons, authoritarian females who must be obeyed. This I will not tolerate.' He muttered this as if to himself. He fixed his eyes upon my face as he continued speaking. 'Miss Jutting, you must regard yourself as fortunate. *I do not approve of women in medicine,* however I cannot, and I will *not* condone unfairness among females; no, this I will *not* tolerate. May I suggest that in due course you send your Matron a letter of thanks. She has given you after all, a most unusual reference, *most unusual.* You will hear from me within the next two weeks. You must keep this conversation confidential, absolutely *confidential.*' Turning his back upon me, his head held high, the dean left me with a strange smile set firmly upon his face.

Within the next fourteen days I received a letter of acceptance signed by the dean, allocating me a Second MB placement within the medical college of St Bartholomew's Hospital; this allowed me to commence my training in clinical medicine, the Second MB course. The study of anatomy, physiology and biochemistry stretched before me. Rapturously I read the letter of acceptance, then, holding it in my hands, I chased our astonished postman down the street, clutching his arms as I chanted: 'I've done it, I've done it, I'm going to hospital at last – I've been accepted.'

The poor man was puzzled, and commiserated with my misfortune at needing to go to hospital. I had to explain that I was going to a teaching hospital to train as a doctor, my dream of a lifetime. My father would, at last, be pleased with me.

It seemed that Matron's reference had miraculously won me that coveted place. I wrote to her, thanking her for her wonderfully supportive reference letter, which allowed me to gain an entry into the medical college of St Bartholomew's Hospital. She never replied.

Chapter 7

I knew that I owed a great deal to University College Hospital for my nursing training. It was not easy at times, and often when faced with sick patients, I had felt very sad. It was a tough, and often difficult way of life for anyone starting at the age of eighteen. The fallout from nursing training was often as high as 20 per cent in some hospitals, though much less so in the London teaching hospitals. But I had survived and the nursing training had undoubtedly strengthened me and made my path ahead seem more straightforward. I felt that I had become a woman, someone in my own right.

I had initially thought to apply to the highly honoured St Bartholomew's Hospital (known as Barts), for a course dealing with the basic sciences, known as the First MB course, which was comprised of biology, chemistry and physics. Successful completion of the First MB would later be followed by studies in anatomy, physiology and biochemistry, the basic part of the Second MB course.

I gave the matter much thought. Money was always short. I had carefully saved twenty pounds over three years of my nursing training, commencing late in 1945. It had seemed a lot of money at the time, but would only serve to pay for one of the three terms even in my local technical college for the First MB. I had not encountered two of these subjects while at school, having only studied biology to matriculation level. The course fees were so much more expensive at Barts. Added to this, train fares to and fro from London would cost me two whole shillings each way. There was no provision of a grant for the first year of training, and I felt it would be unfair to expect my parents to pay those heavy fees for that First MB course at St Bartholomew's Hospital. Finally I forced myself to come to a decision.

Acton Technical College was within walking distance of my home and there was little difficulty in obtaining a place there; only later did I come to sincerely regret my decision. The pass rate for anyone like me, someone who had little or no knowledge of physics or chemistry, was very low. Most of the First MB candidates were those who were having a second attempt following their failure after the two-year A level study of those three subjects. Nevertheless, I was determined to work hard and to pass, having obtained, miraculously it seemed, that vital place in Barts for the Second MB course. It would be my first real introduction to medicine.

In fact, I also had been offered entrance to the medical college of UCH by one of its consultant surgeons. The offer followed that of my acceptance at Barts. I hadn't even applied to UCH. The consultant surgeon was the husband of the patient whom I had nursed within the private wing. I felt truly honoured by his offer, but had to reject it. I expressed my sincere gratitude to that kindly consultant, letting him know that I had already accepted a place at Barts. I felt it would be wise to have a completely fresh start in life and beginning anew in another environment appealed to me. I would be well distanced from Matron, along with the possibility of her anger towards me being transmitted to the senior medical staff. Also, Barts Medical College had an acclaimed reputation.

It seemed like another miracle, but at Acton Technical College I met the Welshman who I had been talking to before my interview at Barts. He lived in Ealing, within a few miles of my home in Acton. Ealing was readily reached using a local bus service. However, my joy in gaining a place for Second MB at Barts was tinged with sadness. Alan, for that was his name, had not been accepted as a medical student at St Bartholomew's Hospital. He felt saddened by the failure. We became good friends, and finally I accepted the offer to meet with him during an evening dance together at the local college. Alan had to teach me how to dance. In my teenage years, I had been a strict Methodist, so had never learnt. It was an entirely new experience. We talked together about his rejection at Barts Hospital.

'I think it was my education,' he said, as we sat down at a table together to catch our breath. 'I got a scholarship to our local grammar school, but none of them had heard of it. I don't think I managed that interview very well.'

Alan never informed the dean at the interview that originally he had intended, before serving in the Royal Air Force, to study engineering, for which he had already been awarded a place at Cambridge University. He never spoke about the excellence of each one of his A grades. It had for him been a difficult interview.

'Were you asked why you decided to take up medicine?' I queried. It was a standard question, yet perhaps one of the most difficult to answer.

'Yes. I told them that God had spoken to me in the desert while I was serving in the forces,' had been Alan's simple but sincere reply. 'Somehow I sensed they were not impressed with my answer.'

Together we managed to laugh.

Soon it became Alan's turn to rejoice. His interview at Christ's College Cambridge for those science studies essential for medicine had been successful. There Alan would study for Part I of his Natural Sciences Tripods, which would, if he passed, allow him to apply for direct entry into the Second MB course, involving the clinical studies, for which his entry to a teaching hospital still remained essential; he had yet to attain a place. Initially Alan decided to take an intermediate Bachelor of Science course in zoology and botany at Acton Technical College; he could cycle there from his home in Ealing. We were not in the same class group at the college, for he had already studied both chemistry and physics, achieving first-class results. He was also highly skilled in mathematics.

I was sure he would soon tire of a woman like me. I was bound to find the physics too much of a challenge, perhaps even impossible. There were rumours that the tutor at my local college was very difficult to follow, especially if one's knowledge of the subject was, like mine, practically non-existent. I did wonder whether I should have undertaken those science studies at Barts in spite of those costly fees that my parents would have been obliged to pay. It had been a difficult decision for me, and it made me wonder whether I had made the wrong one.

I remember very clearly my first visit to Alan's home. There I met his parents, who wanted to be called Edith and George, and together we went to the Sunday service at their Congregational Church. Alan's parents were both born in Wales. His mother was a quiet intellectual woman, often touched with that Celtic melancholy that was, I intuitively knew, so much part of Alan. Both parents were intensely dependent upon each other. Alan's father was a practical man, her staff and her shield, always proud of his wife's scholarship. During that first church service together, my eyes were fixated upon Alan. I became totally oblivious of the singing, the sermon, and even the prayers. My only thoughts were of wonder: that God had found me this treasure. Alan had a fascinating face, full of vitality. His hair was thick, autumn-tinted, which was later bequeathed to his daughter. His eyes were intensely brown, often sparkling, and sometimes pools of sadness; he was undoubtedly handsome. As a youngster, he was called 'Smile', but he had a hidden, pensive side to his nature. He had what I thought to be a typical Welsh body: broad, powerful, of medium height, with very muscular limbs. He sang like an angel.

I was very much aware that during that church service, his father's eyes scrutinised me. It seemed that somehow I had passed the test.

Alan was very anxious about my first visit to his home: it was a large old house that later proved to be a haven for me. Unlike my mother, who was intensely house proud, Edith did not care for chores. In consequence, there was a really hectic rush around at the last minute both by the father and son before I arrived for tea. Sadly they surveyed some of the newly chipped china cups in the tea set reserved for guest visits.

It was of no concern to me. I could have eaten off the floor as long as I sat beside Alan. On an earlier occasion, Alan had made his debut at my parents' home. Mother had set her exquisite Japanese china tea set, along with a silver teapot, on her prized and highly polished dining table. We had then been left alone. Plates had been piled high with homemade cakes. Mother returned later to see if we needed more tea. She was just in time to see her doting daughter, teapot in hand held high, finish pouring the scalding liquid straight onto the newly polished table, her eyes fixated only on the face of the one who had come so suddenly into her life. Vivian Georgina had omitted to set the beautiful Japanese teacup and saucer in place. My mother never remonstrated. Later she passed the incident off with a smile. Alan became her great friend.

In my turn, I came to love his parents, becoming very close to his mother Edith. It was she who became unhappy about her son taking up the proffered place in Cambridge. She wanted him to stay close to the woman he loved. My mother was delighted with my friendship; however, it seemed that my father felt that once committed to Alan I might fail to continue with my training. He was concerned, and expressed his thoughts to my mother. My mother remained loyally committed to Alan.

I continued with my studies with physics, Alan often helping me complete my homework during his holidays. I did not truly understand the class work. I was one of the majority who failed the final examination. I was devastated. I managed both biology and chemistry, but had failed to pass that dreaded physics. In desperation, I wrote to the dean at St Bartholomew's Hospital, along with a plea to be accepted for the medical college First MB course in order to study those basic sciences for yet another year. Almost unbelievably I read the rapid reply from the dean. Again I had been accepted. Once more I would spend a year in the study of those three subjects. My parents were pleased to support me.

I longed with all my being to study with Alan in the same hospital as him; however, St Bartholomew's Hospital had turned him away. No students who were rejected a first time ever had the chance of a second interview. I wondered whether there was any way forward for Alan at Barts at all, or was his attendance there truly an impossible dream? Only two other students within my class of around thirty at Acton Technical College had been successful in securing a place for the Second MB clinical course within a hospital. One included an Indian girl, a friend of mine, who appealed to my father's compassion, because he was convinced that her colour had precluded acceptance. Somehow he managed, through a contact, to obtain a medical student place for her at the Royal Free Hospital. Would that mean, I wondered, that he could also obtain one for Alan. Father firmly expressed his feelings; he could not strike lucky twice. I knew that he did not accord with our eventual liaison. My father worried lest our union together would for me mark the end of further medical studies.

Alan and I consoled each other, and we spent some time rambling together in the summer holidays before the start of term. How vividly I recollect waking up early one morning in my parents' home after a glorious walk on the Eastbourne Downs with Alan on the previous day. I could still sense that wonderful surge of happiness sweeping through my body; already I was missing my man. I felt beyond all doubt that Alan and I were bound together in an everlasting love. I had met the man of my dreams.

I anticipated that our physical separation during term times would be an exquisitely painful operation; with inevitable precision, the surgeon's knife would descend down upon us both, cutting us apart. My vivid imagination pictured the enviably academic females working alongside him: their undoubted intelligence, their many attractions. Would he really want a woman like me as a lifelong partner?

It was the agony of first love, and it was also my last love. Alan had dreams too. He wanted to get married, but we had no money and nothing in our name, absolutely nothing. Initially my father was horrified. He still saw the end of his daughter's career; however, my mother had encouraged our friendship right from the beginning, and in time managed to persuade my father otherwise. My mother offered her engagement ring to us; she wanted it to be worn alongside my wedding ring. It was a two-stone diamond ring, denoting fidelity. Alan's mother also offered her engagement ring to me. I could not turn down her offer; it was made along with her love. I have worn those two rings together for some sixty years. My dear mothers: you remain unforgotten. We were both blessed with loving supportive parents who were our shield in life since our childhood.

Alan and I became betrothed, and in consequence, I entered my first term at Barts, while he started at Christ's College within Cambridge University. We both anticipated hard struggles, but knew we could see each other on the occasional weekend. We did, however, meet together more frequently than originally anticipated. I think I achieved a record. I was the first non-resident betrothed medical student to sleep within the walls of Christ's College. There was always someone away at the weekend, leaving a vacant room. Neither of us would have contemplated sleeping together in the same room. We shared each other's company, and bitter tears were always shed when I was alone once again.

The vision of the China Inland Mission had finally faded into the background when I first met Alan; it was then that I realised that missionary work in China could no longer be contemplated. I did sometimes feel a little guilty, but I firmly believed that Alan and I had been chosen for each other, that was the message that I had received, and in which I firmly believed.

Alan and I had dreams about getting married within the immediate future; two students could surely live together more cheaply than one in the long vacations. Again my beloved parents came to the rescue. Their home was large enough to allow us an upstairs bedroom, and a sitting room. All other facilities would have to be shared. Mother proposed doing all the cooking. And so it came to pass that, with full parental agreement, we planned a date for the marriage; a simple affair for two should not to be long delayed.

The First MB course at St Bartholomew's Medical College seemed entirely different from that of my local technical college. I could understand it, for a start, and in particular, physics seemed somehow to be *related* to the study of medicine. It was taught by Professor Rotblat, a supremely intelligent physicist, who always tried hard to communicate clearly with his class. Sometimes, in despair, he would cry out, 'I do not understand why you do not understand.' Nevertheless he was kind, patient and understanding. Many of the class had similar problems with physics, which comforted me. The chemistry tutor and I got on very well together. I think he really liked me, he always gave me extra help when I asked for explanations. I forged ahead in all of my subjects, even physics. I was even told by my biology tutor during the finals that I was on the shortlist for a Barts scholarship. I did not get it, but somehow that seemed unimportant. My name had at least been put forward. My understanding of those subjects had surely deepened. The teaching had been superb, and I had fully enjoyed learning in that environment.

After I passed the First MB examination at Barts, I was able to start my preclinical course, studying anatomy, physiology and biochemistry. It was then that I put my plan into action. I was both timid and non-assertive by nature, yet I was determined to fight like a lioness for the one I loved; the man I was determined to marry. The dean, the one who had accepted me as a student, had been replaced by another, one who was a consultant surgeon at Barts. It was with him, along with some trepidation, that I sought an interview.

The dean was seated at his desk when I entered his office. He was a powerfully built man with fair hair, and intensely blue eyes. I knew that it was very good of him to allocate his precious time to see me. I was after all only an unknown female student, still in my first term. The dean rose on my entrance; why I never knew. He towered above me; the intensity of his blue eyes bored straight into mine. I had learned in difficult times to look directly upwards into those of my father, and this served me in good stead. I was determined to be a David and face my Goliath. Believing that honesty was the best policy, I explained that 'my boyfriend' – and I used those very words – had been rejected by the previous dean and his committee; that although he had not attended a public school, he had been awarded a scholarship place at Christ's College Cambridge. He wanted more than anything in the world to undertake his clinical studies at Barts. I explained that we both intended to get married; that I had every intention of finishing my training, and continuing with a career, as did my fiancé. In retrospect, I think that many men would have mocked the concept of two medical students anticipating an early marriage while focusing their full attentions upon a medical training.

'Please,' I begged. 'Could my fiancé be given a second interview?' I knew that I was hoping against hope, but I could only but try.

'You really think this could work? Marriage along with medical training?'

'We are both mature students. I completed my nursing training, and my fiancé served in the Royal Air Force. We are absolutely certain that we will succeed.'

I held my head high, staring straight into those blue eyes of the dean.

The silence seemed interminable. Slowly and definitively, the dean, Mr Tuckwell, made his reply; his eyes were fixed firmly upon my face.

'Tell your fiancé to write to me directly, and let me know formally that he wishes to accept a clinical place in this hospital; then at a later date, he must let me know his Cambridge Tripos results.'

Even as he spoke, his hand was stretching out to open the door. It was clearly the end of our discussion and time for me to leave. The door was open, awaiting my departure.

'But what about the interview?' I had stuttered, feeling that I had misunderstood him.

'There is no need for an interview. He has been accepted.'

I hope I said thank you. Dumbstruck, I left the dean with those incredible words still ringing in my ears. The man was a surgeon; by repute, the fastest operator within Barts Hospital, one who came to quick decisions in an emergency. In later years, after qualification, I became his locum houseman for a short period, serving on his ward as a junior. I can still visualise his grand ward rounds. I had to almost take a running pace to keep up with his long strides. I sensed that caused him not a little amusement. I will never forget his kindness; his complete trust in two totally unknown students.

There was a red telephone kiosk just outside the hospital gates. There I made a call to Alan; for both of us it seemed an unbelievable situation. Alan initially thought that I had misunderstood the dean. It took some time to convince him concerning the true situation: Alan had been accepted for a medical training within the walls of St Bartholomew's Hospital, and I had correctly understood what the dean had said. Then my tears came; tears of joy. Alan sent his formal letter of acceptance immediately; for both of us, it seemed an almost unbelievable situation. The memory remains vibrant: Vivian Georgina, almost inarticulate with joy, trying to convince her beloved that all was unbelievably well, that all would end well. We would both become qualified in medicine under the auspices of our highly honoured St Bartholomew's Hospital. It was for each of us a miracle.

Alan studied hard at Cambridge. Later, the master at Christ's College wrote to congratulate Alan: 'On being put in Class 1 of the Natural Sciences Tripos Part 1.' He did in fact top the Cambridge University list. Unbeknown to me, he had also sat the major medical scholarship at Cambridge, which enabled the winner to choose the hospital in which he wanted to undertake his clinical studies. Alan won, and of course chose St Bartholomew's Hospital. It was for him a kind of double guarantee, since the dean had already allocated him a place. It made him feel that he had proved not only to himself, but also to the hospital, that he was worthy of such a place. The dean of the medical college, Mr Tuckwell, was informed. He wrote a letter to Alan which was treasured over the years. It read:

I am very glad to write and inform you that as a result of the combined Hospital Scholarship Examination recently held, you have been awarded the Scholarship offered by this College. We shall expect

you to commence your clinical studies here on 1st
October 1954.

Beloved Alan, it was the first of many scholarships you won at Barts. All our dreams had come true. We could get married, support each other emotionally, and share our lives together within the harbour that was my parents' home. The impossible had been made possible. Together we would train in medicine within the walls of London's most ancient and honoured hospital. Our dream had been realised. My Welshman and I were meant for each other. Our love could not be denied. We were as one.

I scored a number of firsts during my training at Barts. There, I was the first nurse to become accepted as a medical student, the first female student to become engaged while in training and finally Alan and I were the first married students to become qualified while training together.

There were I believe around eleven women, including myself, among the sixty or so students in training together at Barts. All were single at the time, students whose sole ambition was that of becoming qualified in medicine, women who remained devoted to their studies.

Two of these eventually entered the field of psychiatry and another that of paediatrics, while to the best of my knowledge, the remainder became family doctors. There was one student, Sheila, who became a very special friend of mine during our training together; she was also my bridesmaid, and we kept in touch over the years. Sheila too became a family doctor.

My marriage had certainly not been a popular move with some of the teachers at medical college. The disapproval could be sensed. Many assumed that my medical training would end prematurely. Our engagement had been short. While Alan was studying at Cambridge, we missed each other immensely. In fact, we could not see each other every weekend as travel was too expensive and finances would not permit, and in any case, we certainly had our work commitments. Life was always a joy when we met again, but always we had to face yet another agony in parting. It was then that our bitter tears were shed. We both longed for our togetherness. We knew that plans had somehow to be made for the not too distant future.

Finances were our particular problem. Each of us had a grant. Mine was accorded by the local authority, while Alan obtained his from the Royal Air Force where he had served his compulsory enlistment before return-ing to civilian life. Somehow those grants barely seemed to suffice, for we both spent many pounds on precious books. Alan's mother had given me her still treasured engagement ring, but his parents could not support us financially. My own parents had converted their two upper rooms in their house for our sole use, one as a bedroom, and the second as a sitting room. We shared my parents' bathroom; and they also provided the meals. It all helped to support us; we could never have managed financially without my parental support and encouragement.

Marriage meant a more intimate relationship, both on the physical and emotional levels, and so we enjoyed happiness to the full in our times together. I still wept at St Paul's station where we went on our separate ways, Alan having to return to his studies at Cambridge; however, once he had joined me at St Bartholomew's Hospital, the ground seemed so much firmer under our feet.

One problem suddenly came to light, which seemed insurmountable for a short period of time. Proudly I informed my education authority that I had married, and my surname of Jutting was now that of Edwards. In my mind's eye, I had naively anticipated a formal but congratulatory letter. The reply devastated me. It was depressingly cold and to the point. Married women were not eligible for a grant. Mine had therefore been cancelled. My misery was, however, short-lived. It seemed that the Royal Air Force had a more benevolent attitude towards married women. As the student wife of an ex-service man, I could still be maintained on a grant. It was for each of us yet another miracle.

Alan and I had survived yet another storm. The seas became calmer. While I studied the preclinical subjects of anatomy, physiology and biochemistry as an integral part of the London Second MB medical course over an eighteen-month period, Alan studied them to degree level in the Natural Sciences Tripos within Cambridge University, thereby adding six further months of study within his medical training period. I was both happy and pleased when I found that I could not only keep up with the other students, but also, by dint of perseverance and truly long hard hours of study, found myself forging ahead with physiology and biochemistry. I was inspired by Alan, who taught me how to pursue my studies in a logical fashion.

I can still remember feeling upset, even perhaps a little angry, when Alan suggested to me that my nursing training had not been of an academic nature, and therefore I had to learn how to study in order to make the best use of the available time. It was a basic point that had been touched upon during my interview at Barts, which at the time I had chosen to ignore. Nevertheless, as time passed, I had to concede that certainly I needed guidance. Unfortunately, I never really enjoyed the subject of anatomy. Even with the meticulous dissection of a dead body, critically evaluated by our demonstrators, I found it very difficult to visualise tissues and organs, along with the intricate course of arteries, veins and nerves. In contrast, the bones of the skeleton were much easier to memorise. The surfaces could be both clearly viewed and handled. It had always seemed a good idea to take some bones, which Alan and I had purchased, and my *Gray's Anatomy* book along with me to bed each night, burn the midnight oil, and study until the late hours. It worked for me; however, I could only do this while Alan was in his studies at Cambridge. On very many occasions, I would wake up early in the morning to find my hands still clutching the sharpness of a ribcage, or with my chin resting on the solid smoothness of a skull. In retrospect, it was perhaps rather a weird relationship to achieve with the bones of the body; nevertheless it worked. The knowledge obtained was invaluable. Unity with Alan finally followed during the peace of our holiday times together; at the end of the term, joy was fully restored. No longer did I seek the companionship of bones from the human skeleton by night. The learning process had proven successful.

I survived the preclinical course, passing the requisite written, practical and oral tests. My excitement mounted: soon I was going to begin training on the wards. Here I felt that my nursing training should stand me in good stead. I was used to being with patients when they felt at their most vulnerable. I no longer felt embarrassed when holding a patient's hand, no matter if they be male or female, young or old. People undoubtedly feel vulnerable lying on the white anonymity of a hospital bed, with the private parts of their bodies exposed to eyes and probing fingers. I knew how to put them at ease – during my nursing training, I had learnt that empathy and healing go hand in hand.

Medical students were divided into groups that were known as 'firms', each being under the teaching supervision of a consultant serving in his specialist field of medicine. Weekly rounds on patients selected by the consultant for teaching purposes were undertaken by the students during their training. These rounds could be either held in a male or female ward. The consultant's team, working under his wing, comprised of a senior and junior registrar and a senior and junior houseman, who were generally present during these teaching rounds. It was only rarely at that time, that any such post was held by a woman: the title of houseman, the most junior of posts, was what we were called, regardless of sex. Student attendance at the weekly round undertaken by the consultant was imperative; it was an invaluable learning experience, and as such was always fully attended.

Competition for posts under the consultants was always intense, which meant that usually the registrars were not only exceptional from the clinical point of view, but also were generally fine teachers. The junior registrars not only had ward duties to undertake, but also had the prospect of allocating the majority of their free time studying for the examinations of the Royal Colleges, either for medicine, surgery, or obstetrics and gynaecology. Housemen also had a high dependence upon both the senior and junior registrars serving under the consultant, both of whom were available in the ward on a daily basis. Only at a later stage during my medical training did I see a female doctor appointed to the senior post of registrar while serving under a consultant.

My first clinical placement while a student was on a female medical ward. I had been placed in a firm, being the only female among a group of males, all of whom were devoted to rugby. Each student was accorded three patients, while new admissions were allocated on arrival. Medical histories had to be recorded, alongside the results following the student's full physical examination. None of us would admit to being apprehensive, but I think that even the toughest among us felt nervous.

Our sister had a gimlet eye. She treated us all like errant teenagers liable to run amok. Her voice boomed out instructions down the length of the ward at regular intervals. Woe betide any male student taking an undue length of time behind a screen during his examination of a female patient: a chaperone was always required, which involved removing a nurse from her other ward duties. Sister could always find other more useful duties to occupy the time of her nurses. Medical students, in particular males, only served to upset the ward routine, thereby wasting not only her valuable time, but also that of her nurses. Sister always felt free to express herself. 'Nurse, lunches are about to be served'; or 'Nurse, it is time for the drug round *now*' often disrupted the time a male student spent with his patient.

Little did some of the patients realise the extent of the students' ignorance during their early introduction to life on the ward, nor did they sense the initial embarrassment experienced by some males being obliged to ask some intimate questions regarding a female patient's symptoms. A woman in her early student training could also suffer similar embarrassment while undertaking a clinical session with a male patient; for me it was a much easier matter. My nursing experiences with male patients allowed me a much more confident approach. I enjoyed these sessions.

One sister was of great help during our training, introducing us to the patients with the most obvious clinical signs, such as a lump in the breast, jaundice, or a distended abdomen. For medical students, it was a sound introduction to clinical medicine. Seated proudly at her desk, Sister had made herself known to us on our first day on her ward, her brown eyes remaining firmly fixed upon us all: 'You must never forget that you are privileged to be here. You are learning on *my patients*.'

There was another sister who often made male students feel embarrassed and at times humiliated. She considered them to be a trial, a useless adjunct to the ward. It made them long for qualification; as for me, I was ignored, except when leaving a patient after performing a physical examination. The neatness of my 'hospital corners' on the bed sheets was noticed. Nevertheless, I always refrained from informing the staff about my nursing background. Sister always laid down the law on her female ward, making all students leave the bed in a pristine condition following their consultation with the patient. I thought this a positive plan, for it made the students understand that patients had not only to be made comfortable following their consultation, but their bed had to be left looking tidy. This sister also insisted that students should only undertake surgical dressings when supervised by a senior nurse. Again, woe betide any male student emitting raucous laughter while examining a female; her nurses and patients had to be protected from such coarseness at all times.

I often spent my free time visiting my ward, being allowed to examine those patients recently admitted who displayed interesting 'lumps and bumps'. The sisters varied in their approach to students, but I always made sure that I thanked them for their kind services. It was a major responsibility running a busy ward, involving not only the care of patients but also the supervision of nurses during their training period. A ward sister carried heavy responsibilities.

Each medical student had to make sure the ward sister's permission was sought before the examination of patients within her ward. We also had to make sure that patients did not resent an intrusion upon their time. Anyone with what was termed an 'interesting' physical sign, such as an abdominal or breast tumour, was often inundated with these requests. Nevertheless, I was never confronted by a patient refusing such a request, although the nursing staff would always do their best to protect a patient from too many such examinations during the course of the day. I soon learnt to find out whether any new patients had been admitted overnight, and also whether they had already been visited by a member of the senior medical staff; such visits enabled me to peruse their medical notes, thereby checking both on my own physical examination and also my own diagnostic skills. It taught me to be self-critical and always made me feel humble. There was always more learning to be achieved.

I will never forget one male patient in his early twenties. He was the first patient from whom I took a history, while serving on a male ward. Recently arrived, he looked somewhat taken aback when he realised he was to be examined by a female. I had some spare time, so I tried to chat to him pleasantly before asking any questions.

'Just what made you come into hospital?'

There was silence. Then he started talking. 'I have a German Shepherd dog, an Alsatian. He is a pedigree dog, and an absolute beauty. He is also a fantastic guard dog. I am considering entering him in for Crufts. Have you got a dog?'

I was feeling puzzled, but fortunately decided to be patient, and to bide my time.

'I could not live without my dog, my Rex. They are quite an expense and a responsibility too, especially with the vet's fees, travelling to shows and kennel fees if one is away.' He sighed thoughtfully, the frowns on his forehead deepening.

I listened while he told me all about the wonders of his dog Rex. Alan and I had always longed for a dog.

The patient continued. 'I took him to the vet just for a routine examination and I couldn't believe it when he told me that he could only feel just one testis in the scrotum when of course there should be two.'

Puzzled, I was longing to repeat my question: 'Just why did *you* come into hospital?' Again I remained silent, and listened.

The young man looked across at me and repeated: 'Only one testis. It was such a shock. You see, my Rex had to have an operation.'

At last I began to comprehend what he was trying to tell me. His alarm was raised when he too had located only one testis in his own scrotum. These generative organs evolve in the abdomen within the early embryonic stage, but normally descend externally before birth. Since cancer could develop within a testis retained within the abdomen, an operation has to be undertaken in order to bring the aberrant organ down to the cooler environment of the scrotal sac. In that particular incident, the patient owed a lot to his dog.

The grand round was initially quite terrifying to most of the medical students. The consultant, along with his team of senior and junior registrars and housemen, would sweep into the ward on a twice-weekly basis. He would be met by a graciously smiling sister and her senior staff nurse, and ushered around the ward like visiting royalty. The waiting medical students would jump to attention, and silently gather around the white-coated team. Under Sister's eagle eye, the patients remained quiet during the consultant's round; it was considered to be a very important event.

The consultant's visit, along with that of his team, was designed to be a teaching round for students, as well as serving to monitor his patients. Certainly it was a privileged learning experience for each one of us. Students were assigned patients, from whom they had to take a detailed medical history, as well as undertaking a thorough medical examination. Any one of the students could be selected to 'present their case' during the consultant's round, which meant producing a well-researched list of the differential diagnoses needing to be considered; this had to be followed by cogent reasoning as to why a particular diagnosis had finally been reached by the student. It was a tremendous learning experience both for the student presenting the case and those of us who were listening. It took a little time for the consultant on our initial teaching rounds to call me to task. He was clearly not highly in favour of females taking an active role during his rounds.

While a student, I was allocated an elderly lady who had been admitted from the casualty department on the previous day. One of the nurses kindly enclosed the patient with screens, allowing the patient and I some privacy. The registrar had already assessed her, but she was now made available as a learning experience to students. I felt quite nervous when facing her, wondering whether I was really capable of presenting that consultant with a correct diagnosis. Already two of the male students had failed in their attempt to clarify the medical diagnosis leading to their patient's hospital admission. In nearly all of the cases, the patient had, prior to their hospital admission, initially been seen and examined by their family doctor, then referred onwards to the consultant's outpatient department for further investigation and treatment, along with hospital admission if considered necessary. I knew that the family doctor's letter, addressed to the consultant, could often be very helpful in clarifying the clinical situation. I had no such letter to peruse, since my patient had collapsed in the street, and from there been taken by ambulance directly to the hospital's casualty department.

There were certainly quite a few occasions when a patient was admitted directly into a ward from the casualty department, not having seen a consultant on any previous outpatient appointment. This was probably more common when there was a surgical problem, such as a serious body injury incurred following a road traffic accident. Disease of the blood vessels relating to the brain tissue remains one of the most common causes of disability or death within the developed world; collapse of the patient either in the home, or at work, could lead to hospital admission on an emergency basis.

Seating myself beside my patient, I told her that I was a medical student, and requested her patience while I asked some questions relating to the medical background of her family. We then had a discussion concerning the various medical problems that had arisen during her own lifetime, in particular, those relating to her admission to Barts. I think the woman, whose name was Louise, soon felt at ease with me. Initially her face lit up with a smile when she saw '*a woman doctor*' approaching; she went on to explain that since childhood, she had always felt nervous in the presence of men. The seventy-year-old patient told me that her two younger brothers had died at the relatively early ages of fifty-five and fifty-eight years. Each had appeared to be fit, yet both had the history of a sudden collapse while at work, then dying a few days later following hospital admission. The father of the family had a similar history, having collapsed while at work, and dying at the age of forty-five years. Apparently her mother had not experienced any unusual medical problems; she had died peacefully in her sleep at the age of ninety-two.

I wondered whether I was looking for an obscure congenital disease within the family. I considered my knowledge to be so limited. It transpired that Louise had regarded herself as reasonably fit until the age of sixty. Fatigue and some recent loss of memory troubled her; and she had been wondering whether it would be wise for her to move to a much smaller home. She was a widow, living alone, both daughters married with families of their own. She had suffered a sudden collapse followed by a temporary loss of consciousness, which had lasted for some sixty minutes. It had led to her hospital admission. The woman had been out on a shopping spree at the time.

I undertook what I felt to be a careful physical examination of the patient, and could detect no apparent abnormalities. Her lung fields were clear, and there seemed to be no abnormal 'lumps and bumps' that could be detected during bodily palpation.

I was puzzled. The patient interrupted my cogitations, telling me that the consultant had told her that an ECG would be undertaken.

'I wrote those letters down while he was talking. Is that an operation?'

The patient sounded very concerned while she questioned me. I explained with a smile that it was a very simple procedure: just a photographic recording of the electrical variations occurring during contraction of the heart muscle.

As I examined her further, I became concerned. During my initial examination of the patient, I had applied my stethoscope to the chest wall in order to examine the lungs, and had also carefully listened to her heart beat. I could detect no abnormality either in the heart rate or the air entry into the lungs. Just what had I missed? Was there perhaps a heart lesion; an abnormality in the heart beat that I had failed to detect? I thought I had made a meticulous and complete examination of the other parts of the body; so what was the diagnosis?

Louise noticed my worried frown. 'I'm having quite a few tests: blood, urine, chest X-ray and of course they seem to be taking my blood pressure regularly. I understand that it was very high when I was first admitted. I suppose the doctor can make sure that the medication he prescribed for lowering my blood pressure is working while I'm still here in the ward. I understand I will probably have to be on these drugs for the rest of my life, just to keep my blood pressure within normal limits. I don't mind, as long as the drugs continue to work. I'm so relieved. I do not think that an operation will be necessary. That's what always worried me. I have always had a fear of hospitals and operations.'

I looked up in amazement. Of course, I had failed to take the woman's blood pressure. Was that her major problem? When I then took her blood pressure, it was at an acceptable level, and with a smile, I reassured my patient that her blood pressure was fine. She had been on medication for hypertension for some twenty-four hours. I remained puzzled: was essential hypertension the diagnosis?

The patient continued with her history. 'The consultant used a strange word. I didn't really understand what he meant. He mentioned the word "essential hypertension" while he was telling me that my blood pressure was too high. Perhaps there is something odd about our family genes but how could a high blood pressure be "essential", it just doesn't make sense to me. Does it mean that I will have it to the end of my life? That it cannot be properly treated, yet it is "essential" for my well-being? I just do not understand. Tell me: exactly what is meant by "essential hypertension"?'

I clasped my patient's hand. 'It is diagnosed when an underlying cause for your raised blood pressure just cannot be found, and that occurs in the majority of cases. Only then it is termed "essential hypertension". However, it can be treated, and kept under control, provided you keep up with your prescribed medication. You will need to go to the clinic sessions where a nurse can take your blood pressure on a regular basis, in order to make absolutely sure that it is held within the normal limits. There are different drugs available that will lower the blood pressure. Your blood pressure is now within normal limits, so clearly you are on the right medication.' I spoke slowly, pressing the patient's hand in an attempt to relieve her anxiety. 'Your medication is working, so you can relax.'

'Surely I can test my own blood pressure? I will buy a machine from our pharmacy, once I am at home again.'

I was impressed with the concept of patients being taught to record their own blood pressure, it could surely be a life-saving procedure, and a visit to the family doctor could always be undertaken if there were any concerns. Patient self-measurement of her blood pressure seemed a sound idea to me; however, I suggested that it should still be checked by a nurse or doctor regularly, so records could be maintained. I advised her to talk to her family doctor about the matter. Perhaps he should give the final decision.

My patient had preserved my honour, and I proceeded to present my findings to the consultant in an assured manner, suggesting that the correct diagnosis was that of a 'transient ischaemic attack, or TIA', due to a raised blood pressure. I had learnt much during my examination of his patient. When I had finally finished presenting my case he grunted his confirmation. My confidence was buoyed up, and my thanks were due to my patient. After that diagnosis, I became an accepted member of the team working within that consultant's ward round, along with those male students.

It also left me with the realisation that untreated essential hypertension remained a problem, and came to the belief that its measurement should not be neglected, particularly in the elderly. I did wonder: should clinics be set up on a national basis, possibly being attached to the family doctors' surgeries, whereby patients within a certain age group had their blood pressure recorded on a regular basis by a nurse? I was uncertain as to exactly what age this should start, but presumably it would involve those who were retired, since the incidence of both stroke and cardiovascular disease (that relating to blood vessels surrounding the heart) was known to increase with age and males were more at risk than females of essential hypertension. During my training, I learnt that some medical people monitored their own blood pressure on a regular basis. I even remember being told by a consultant physician that one family doctor always advised her older patients to do the same, having told them that the instrument for measuring blood pressure, the sphygmometer, could readily be purchased from one of the major pharmaceutical firms. It had impressed me at the time.

I clearly remember another patient who had been admitted to hospital following the discovery of a very high blood pressure by her family doctor. Emily, an elderly lady, initially seemed reluctant to give me her medical details during my first visit; she appeared to find it an embarrassment that her family doctor had not only taken her blood pressure, but also had carried out a full medical examination, including the examination of her breasts. Fortunately she had accepted her doctor's advice, and with great reluctance, finally agreed to submit herself to hospital admittance following what her family doctor diagnosed as a 'transient ischaemic attack'. After my initial examination of Emily, I realised that a second visit was essential, which I made later in the day. It was only that she reluctantly revealed a further problem, one which she had failed to mention even to her own doctor. Emily had suffered from severe constipation for months, along with some episodes of bleeding from her 'back passage'. She confessed to being too embarrassed to mention that particular problem even to her family doctor. Emily listened carefully to me, as I tried to impart the importance of listening to the specialist medical advice so readily obtainable at Barts, to which she finally agreed. Eventually she agreed to proceed with an operation. Fortunately the surgery involving the removal of a cancerous tumour within the bowel was successful, and the patient was eventually discharged into the care of a rest home.

Undoubtedly my nursing training stood me in good stead. I even began to wonder whether every medical student should for a limited period be allocated some nursing duties on a ward as an integral part of their training. Nurses learn to listen, and have the privilege of acting as a chaperone during a male doctor's medical examination of a female. A patient always seemed to react positively to the sympathy shown by someone prepared to listen attentively. This allowed a sick and vulnerable individual to discuss intimate symptoms without undue embarrassment. During my nursing training, I had always taken a great deal of interest in listening to a patient's symptoms, and also in asking the attending doctor questions relating to those symptoms.

Medical students at my beloved Barts Hospital could, on a voluntary basis, attend Saturday morning outpatient sessions. There was no problem if one lived within the medical college, but for others such as me it meant travel, along with further expenditure on fares. Nevertheless, I always attended, and found these sessions to be absolutely invaluable. There is one particular surgeon who remains unforgotten.

Mr Ellison Nash was an excellent teacher. He was a muscular man with the habit of pursing his lips if displeased. A devoted Christian, his patients' welfare was his paramount concern. He also believed it was his duty to teach. He had developed a singular style of teaching that was certainly demanding and also dogmatic, and eminently suitable for medical students, particularly one such as myself. The popularity of his surgical outpatient sessions was always assured among the medical students, despite being held on Saturday mornings.

Clinical students had no holidays, and continued seeing patients both in casualty and on the wards. Alan was still studying for his degree, and during the university vacation was obliged to work alone within my parents' home. We did after all have our own little nest upstairs. A brilliant idea came to my mind like a bolt from the blue. I had tried to prepare the way by asking several leading, and I hoped, some thoughtful questions during one of Mr Ellison Nash's Saturday morning surgical outpatient sessions. I then approached the surgeon following the end of his session.

'I am married to a Cambridge student, sir. He will be coming to Barts for his clinical training. Sir, could he attend your Saturday sessions? It would be such a marvellous preparation for him, please, sir.' The words tumbled out incoherently in my nervousness.

Steady brown eyes looked into mine. Heavy black brows beetled across his furrowed forehead. There was silence. The surgeon's eyes were fixed upon my face. Silently I stood there, awaiting an answer. I wondered if I had overstepped the mark. I feared a scathing comment. The surgeon believed in honesty at all costs. Surely the silence had to be broken.

'He would not be a nuisance, sir; he is a mature student,' I said timidly. I feared a coming storm, but instead there was a smile.

'Then he can come along next Saturday. Make sure to sit in the front row so he can see and hear me clearly.'

Stern though he seemed at times, that surgeon was both kind and understanding in his approach to students.

Following Mr Nash's invitation, Alan and I had duly sat down in the front row, so we had a full view of the patient, and could clearly hear the surgeon's interrogation, and witness his clinical examination. In order to clarify one of his points, I whispered softly into Alan's ear. The surgeon turned round abruptly. He looked fiercely at the faces in the front row, focusing his eyes upon a tall male student seated by Alan's side.

'Your name, and was it you talking?' His voice was raised in anger.

'Edwards, sir. No, I was not talking.'

Mr Nash turned to my husband. 'Was it you? And your name?'

The reply was hesitant. 'Not me, sir. My name is Edwards.'

Brown eyes perused my face. Had he not recognised me?

'And you: was it you causing the interruption? And your name?'

'Yes, it was me. I was explaining about…' I stopped when I saw his forehead furrow into deep ridges. Then I added without any thought. 'My name is Edwards, sir.'

I suddenly realised that the surgeon thought that we were mocking him. Some of the students smiled, and others chuckled; then there emerged a synchronous and sustained low laughter from among that audience of students. It was cut short when the surgeon turned his back upon everyone. Clearly he was not amused. However, he maintained his sense of humour in front of his patient, and within a minute had resumed his talk. It was an odd coincidence that Alan and I were sitting beside another student named Edwards. He clearly considered it to be an amusing incident. I had of course succeeded in offending the surgeon while sitting along-side my husband in that front row. Alan and I faced our surgeon after his teaching session had been completed. I apologised profusely, explaining that there truly had been three students with the same surname sitting in adjoining seats. I then introduced Alan, reminding him that Alan was my husband, to whom he had given permission to attend. Finally we both thanked him for giving us that privilege. We all stood there in silence. I felt fearful.

Suddenly our surgeon turned his face towards us and chuckled. 'A not uncommon name,' he murmured, smiling. 'See you both next week.'

Our hearts were raised. We would still both be welcomed to attend his superb teaching sessions; it was for both of us an enormous privilege, one to which we became devoted, there being so much for each of us to learn.

There seemed to be a consensus among some consultants concerning the career structure of students. Some seemed to assume that after qualification in general medicine, further postgraduate training in one of the specialities such as surgery, medicine, obstetrics and gynaecology was an important aim. My impression at that time, and I could have been wrong, was that there were some consultants who had come to the decision that students aiming to become general practitioners were in the process of falling down the academic ladder. In consequence, the acquisition of esoteric knowledge was encouraged. Barts, like other London teaching hospitals, admitted patients not only from the local area but also seemed to select patients with unusual diseases from all parts of the country; patients who had been born in other parts of the world were also sometimes seen within the ward. The tuition was superb. Barts consultants were highly specialised.

Mr Ellison Nash, however, steered away from the esoteric. He had a particular concern in teaching students about common diseases and his straightforward diagnoses were invaluable. Each student had to approach the patient as if he or she was a caring family doctor, and then undertake a meticulous medical history. This was followed by a careful clinical examination in an attempt to solve the patient's problems. There was security in the knowledge that the patient could always be referred to a specialist consultant by the family doctor should further medical guidance be required. Thus he emphasised the importance of family doctor intervention. In the preservation of patient health, there always had to remain that vital link between both the consultant and the family doctor. This attitude of mind stood all who learned and inwardly digested, in remarkably good stead within the final student examinations. The missed diagnosis of an endocrine or glandular disease such as diabetes mellitus could result in a lifelong disease for the patient, or even fatality.

Alan had achieved a first-class degree from Cambridge. Even before he finally qualified, he had decided that surgery was for him the only possible career. Alan lacked surety in himself, and also confidence in his educational background. The fact that some of the medical students came from public schools made him feel insecure. However, the academic distinctions he achieved while at Cambridge soothed his spirit.

At home, once Alan was studying at Barts, life could become difficult as we both worked long hours, each with varying off-duty periods, which did not necessarily coincide. Exhaustion often followed, and we learnt to support our beloved partner through all our difficulties. During his bachelor days, Alan had always got out of bed just in time for breakfast, using practically all of the evening in order to learn from the large tomes essential for medical studies. Supper for him had always been in the very late evening. Before marriage, I had always risen very early, starting my work well before breakfast, while using all the hours available before a reasonably timed evening meal for study purposes. We somehow learnt to work together, which was not always easy, especially over the weekends. I decided to compromise, and change my study time, starting at nine o'clock in the mornings, rather than commencing at 6 a.m. I also geared myself to work along with Alan until later in the evening. During our precious weekends together, Alan made himself rise earlier, rather than indulging in a sleep till mid-morning.

Together we studied as a team. He taught me to read critically, analysing the sentences, while trying to look at ideas from the first principle point of view.

Medicine was my forte: I found the study of the presentation of bodily diseases fascinating. I knew it was vitally important to elucidate all the symptoms experienced by the patient and that a very careful medical history of the patient had always to be obtained. It was also very important to question whether there was any family history of disease, along with that of any previous operative procedures. Congenital heart disease usually seemed to present itself during the first year of life; however, symptoms such as heart failure, heart murmurs and irregular heart beat more often presented themselves in later infancy, childhood and adolescence, while also occurring during adult life. The signs of a particular disease could be displayed during careful observation and examination of the patient's body.

Medical students had much to learn. The prolonged smoking of cigarettes could cause lung cancer, so it was absolutely essential to undertake meticulous examination of the lungs with the use of a stethoscope; absence of air entry could indicate the presence of a lung disease. Careful clinical examination of the body, along with the gentle palpation of its various areas could reveal not only the presence of abnormal swellings, but could also produce pain. All such observations had to be carefully noted on admission, while follow-up examinations were always made during the inpatient stay. Various clinical tests, such as those of urine and blood, along with various procedures such as X-rays, could be arranged following the patient's examination by the doctor. Because surgery involved operative procedures, it required a specialised training followed by the final examination, success of which was awarded with the FRCS; the Fellowship of the Royal College of Surgeons.

Although Alan and I became attached to different 'firms', we nevertheless got together in our free times, always attending the teaching rounds where the tuition was outstanding. One medical senior registrar in particular could barely accommodate the numbers of listening and participating students within his ward. A physician, he was highly skilled in investigative and diagnostic procedures, along with treatment involving the use of medication. His teaching abilities were superlative. Our registrar was already a member of the Royal College of Physicians.

I tended to lack self-confidence during the grand teaching rounds. Alan always encouraged me to join in with the debate, armed as I was with the long lists of differential diagnoses as set out in my wonder book, *French's Index of Differential Diagnosis*. We examined patients together, which meant that we did not have to request a chaperone; this always pleased the busy ward sisters and their nurses. We would find out which patients had heart murmurs, or fascinating lumps and bumps. We would then slip around the ward together. The patients never seemed to mind, in fact, many liked a little chat, always somewhat surprised to find that we were a married couple. It gave them a real sense of reassurance during their physical examination.

'Thought all young people lived together these days,' murmured one old lady with a pleased smile. 'Good to see a young married couple.'

Alan and I always took great care in the examination of breasts during our introduction to a new patient. The presence of a suspected breast tumour in a patient always involved medical concern; careful clinical evaluation along with test procedures always followed. When considered essential, surgery was offered to the patient. One of the consultants always advised female students to self-palpate their breasts on a regular basis. One of my friends, while in her medical training at another London hospital, always performed her own breast palpation; she discovered such a 'lump'. Her cancer was in a very early stage and the tumour was successfully removed. The consultant's advice brought to mind a patient I had examined while working within a male ward on a previous occasion. I had palpated an elderly gentleman's breasts, and had felt a swelling in the left breast. It was found to be a cancerous tumour, and was surgically removed. I was told that such tumours were rare in men.

There were many scholarships available to Barts students, and Alan tried to encourage me to sit for them. My response was quite negative. 'Not me. There are some really brilliant chaps in my set. I have no chance at all.'

'It's a good practice for the finals, and will make you selective in your reading. It does not cost you anything, and it would be a very good experience.' Alan always offered support and encouragement, and was very patient with his obstinate wife. Following much persuasion, I finally agreed.

Scholarships seemed an impossible attainment to me. Initially I felt overwhelmed. Alan and I shared our books, and I learned to value the red biro marks made on every page of my precious tome *French's Index of*

Differential Diagnosis. Due to the time Alan spent while studying at Cambridge University, I was some months ahead of my husband; consequently the opportunity to enter for those Barts' clinical scholarships came to me first. Urged on by Alan, I put my name forward for the Roxburgh Skin Prize, and the Kirke Gold Medal in medicine. I studied till the late hours, and also examined many patients. To my great astonishment, I was awarded the dermatology scholarship. I was also given what was termed the 'Prox. Access to the Kirke Gold Medal in Medicine'; the student who won it was the man Edwards who had sat alongside Alan and myself during one of Mr Nash's surgical sessions. He was an Oxford University student, being some months ahead of me in clinical experience, which gave me great encouragement. However, my pleasure was rudely deflated when one of the ablest men in my set said with a smile: 'If I had known *you* were going to get that placement, I would have put my name forward too.'

Some of the cleverest men, at least judged by the internal examination results, had decided against having a try at these prestigious awards. I understood the fear of failure and loss of face well. I wouldn't have sat the tests had not Alan put a gun to my head, forcing his wife to march onwards into battle. One certainly learnt a lot from such experiences, and I realised that I owed a lot to Alan's patience and perseverance with his ever-obstinate wife.

Time passed quickly. My clinical knowledge was slowly built up during my own training period; however, the time seemed to pass very quickly. Examinations always made me feel apprehensive, and I had to learn to speak clearly and with confidence. On many occasions I still felt myself to be a humble nurse. I forced myself to dispel that image, and to remember that my dream had come true. I was actually in the throes of learning within the field of medicine, along with the dream that one day I might even achieve qualification.

Our clinical and oral final examinations were undertaken in other London teaching hospitals, while the written papers were taken in Senate House, sited in London. The papers seemed reasonable; however, I did not think there was much of a chance in attaining distinction level. I still had some hopes, but was never a good judge of my own efforts. It was the clinical examinations that inspired most fear. There were stories recounted by the students of brilliantly written papers being undermined by errors within those clinical trials.

In a hospital strange to them, the student was faced with a consultant-selected patient from whom they had to obtain a medical history, following which a clinical examination had to be made The student then had to face a detailed questioning by the examiner, and present the final diagnosis. I had never forgotten the times when I had acted as a chaperone for male medical students facing their finals when in my nurse training at University College Hospital. It had been a very useful experience. While a medical student, I had also volunteered to act as a chaperone for candidates aspiring for the prestigious Fellowship of the Royal College of Surgeons. In this, my sex was a real advantage. I, along with two of my female friends, were enviously regarded by the male students. We could watch an experienced candidate take a history from a patient, while we acted as a chaperone, and observe the physical examination being undertaken. We also had the privilege of listening to their learned discussions following these procedures. It was a privilege for each one of us, a time for learning, an education in medicine.

'It is so unfair. Gives you females a real advantage over us chaps.'

'Life is unfair,' had been my reply. 'For one time in our life, sex discrimination is in our favour.'

Strangely enough, I found most of the final examinations much less of an ordeal than originally anticipated; this was all due to Alan's constant encouragement. I had attended many teaching rounds, and discussed many a patient's history with my husband, so that I must have been reasonably well primed. However, I nearly panicked in the final pathology practical examination. I was handed a pot containing a sturdy upright projection, and asked to discuss the possible disease, along with the final diagnosis. My mind literally became a blank as I stared into the expressionless face of the elderly bald-headed examiner. Carefully I perused the pot. I could see a small darkly coloured tumour at the tip of the wretched thing. I felt quite sick. Surely it was the penis. I almost said: 'A malignant melanoma of the penis.'

Why I desisted I never knew. Was Alan sending out special thought waves to me? I inspected the contents of the pot closely, being beset with the intuition that all was not well with my diagnosis. Suddenly, through the preserving fluid, I noted the presence of a nibbled nail at the top of the mystery specimen.

'A malignant melanoma in the nail bed of a finger,' I said with confidence, before elaborating on the various approaches in treatment. I could so easily have failed, being overwhelmed by an unreasoning anxiety that urged me to make a rapid diagnosis. Never before had I seen such a swollen finger, even in a male.

There was a slight stretching of the lips, the semblance of a smile on the face of the examiner, and an almost whimsical look in the depths of his eyes. I did wonder. Perhaps other aspiring candidates had fallen by the wayside.

The finals in surgery were those I dreaded most; one particular examiner was said to have a severe style, especially with female students. One dear friend was such a victim. An extremely able student, she had always performed well in her examinations, both written and practical. However, she ended up in tears following her clinical examination of the patient when she was questioned as to the diagnosis by the surgeon. She had made a classic misdiagnosis, following which she had suggested a procedure on the patient. Sternly she had been advised that this would most likely end in a fatality if undertaken within the family doctor's surgery, which had been her suggested procedure. We later learnt that the patient had a hernia involving the protrusion of a small part of the intestine into the scrotal sac. My friend had mistakenly suggested the swelling was due to a collection of fluid around the testis, which could be successfully withdrawn by the family doctor, while using a sterile procedure.

The knowledge that one has failed in at least one major subject does not fill a candidate with the confidence so essential when several other final examinations have still to be taken. I just hoped that I would not be assessed by this particular surgeon.

My worst fears were confirmed as I stepped into the examination room. I was met by a tall muscular man with piercing blue eyes. A thick thatch of fuzzy red-gold hair flopped over a wide forehead. All the students knew his description. Over six feet, he towered over my five foot three inches. In my agitation, I dropped my small handbag, which I had slung over my arm. The clasp burst open, spilling the contents, which included a powder compact, and lipstick, along with a pen and a diary; they rattled and rolled over the tiled flooring. I decided that I had already failed, as I started to crawl on my hands and knees towards one of the corners of the room in an attempt to retrieve the contents of my handbag. Suddenly there was a loud thump. Two heads had collided together, for that mighty man had also got down on his hands and knees. Dazed, I looked up into his eyes. There was a sudden sound of explosive laughter – from him.

The incident succeeded in relaxing me. I was directed to my first patient, the so-called 'long case'. The candidate was expected to extract a detailed history, make a full examination, and present a final diagnosis following full consideration of all the possibilities.

'Made me laugh, that it did,' said the elderly male patient. 'Saw you both bumping your heads together on the floor. Not laughed so much for a good long time. Made me feel so much better.'

I took a detailed history. The symptoms were vague and ambiguous: there was an ill-defined pain in the upper abdomen, along with a loss of weight. The physical examination was equally puzzling. There appeared to be no abnormal signs, apart from some slight tenderness in the upper abdomen. There were no lumps or bumps on the skin, nor yet any apparent enlargement of the internal organs, none that I was able to palpate.

The old man laughed. Then he whispered: 'Got them all scratching their heads, that it did: went to my local hospital and the doctors there sent me here. Couldn't make head nor tail of anything.'

I stopped him, suddenly realising that I had failed to ask about any tests that had been undertaken. The patient made some vague references to blood tests, 'tubes down my throat', and X-rays, but with no specific details. I was beginning to panic, until he started talking very softly, his gnarled hand over mine.

'Got lots of visits, you know, when the specialists came with their students. Everyone was just talking all about me, lovely to listen. Doctors crowded round my bedside; even included a professor from Africa. He seemed to know what was wrong with me, I find it difficult to remember his words... retro...retro peri...tumour... so difficult to remember. His words didn't make sense, not to me.'

'Retroperitoneal tumour?' I questioned, suddenly feeling less muddled.

'That's right; that was it. Must have heard that word a thousand times since he came. I was examined by lots more doctors, all wanting to talk to me. I heard them use the words, "cancer of the pancreas". Heard the doctors say I'll get yellow near the end. I'm not yellow yet, so maybe more time before I go.' The old man squeezed my hand and sighed. 'I know I've had my chips. Why me? But I've lost my missus and life isn't the same without her, so I've got to believe I'll see her again, and maybe sooner than I think.'

The time allocated to me was nearly finished; however, I felt I had surfaced through those deep waters, and could at last draw a deep breath.

'Perhaps you should not have told me all about your illness.'

My patient cut across me. 'First time I've laughed for weeks, seeing that great surgeon crawling on the floor like a small kid. *Don't you worry, doctor.* Not a word said to the other students, only you. Mum's the word. My missus would have liked you. Good luck, doctor, and don't forget: it's me pancreas.'

It was the first time that I had been called 'doctor'. Surely it was a good omen? Was I wrong not to divulge that I had been given the diagnosis? I did not have much time to muse upon the matter. The surgeon swept into the screened-off area.

'Handbag safe?' he inquired solemnly.

I assured him that it was safe. I then went on to give a concise history, emphasising the difficulties over the apparent lack of physical signs. I produced an impressive list of the kind of investigations that would be essential, along with my final decision upon the diagnosis.

My old patient continued smiling, while the surgeon grunted his approbation. I was then hustled onwards to assess six short cases. It was a record number. Many of the candidates had around four. Silently I blessed Mr Nash, whose surgical outpatients teaching rounds both Alan and I had assiduously attended. Smiling, I thanked my patient, feeling that it was all due to him that I had somehow miraculously managed to present the correct diagnosis. I felt truly blessed.

Chapter 8

In 1956, I had at last completed the long years of study, and all those final examinations had at last been taken. Had my impossible dream of becoming a qualified doctor been realised at last? The waiting time for results seemed so prolonged. Some of the students were sure that they had failed, while others felt certain of success. My personality would never enable me to be sure of my results. Some of the students went on holiday, while others browsed through the *British Medical Journal* looking for likely posts. Those who had won a coveted internal scholarship approached the Barts consultants, for traditionally such awards were a passport to successful achievement of a house post within the hospital. Each newly qualified doctor had to become registered before being allowed to practise; in consequence two house posts, each of six months' duration, had to be undertaken, one in general medicine, and the other either in surgery or obstetrics and gynaecology.

There was a junior post open for application under the consultant in dermatology for which I could have applied, since I had been awarded the scholarship. Unfortunately, the post did not count towards registration. Had I taken it, I would have had to wait for a further six months before I could apply to become registered. I decided not to delay formal registration, and consequently did not make an application. In retrospect, I think I made a mistake. At that time, women were rarely given the privilege of house posts within Barts, so had I been accepted for the houseman post in dermatology, it could possibly have served as the 'way in through the back door'. Six months' service within a ward devoted to patients with problems involving the skin, under a consultant who never lost his interest in general medicine, would have been an excellent introduction to service within the hospital. My decision not to wait for a further six months to attain registration was costly. I gave up any possible chance of ever attaining a house post within Barts. I knew that it was extremely unlikely for me as a woman to be considered for any other speciality. I did not want to work in surgery; a medical post had always been my dream. I finally forced myself to face the consultant obstetrician.

'Would you consider me, sir? Could I apply for your junior houseman post?'

The obstetric consultant looked down upon me as he replied, 'I suggest, Mrs Edwards, that you go and raise a family. Go and have a baby.'

Those were his precise words. They seemed so judgemental. It seemed of prime importance to that consultant that my goal in life was to fulfil my role as a woman and nothing more. Service within my beloved Barts was not obtainable; the door was closed.

The time came for all the students to congregate at the Senate House in Mallet Street, London. There a list would be displayed of all the successful candidates who had taken the Bachelor of Medicine and Bachelor of Surgery final examinations, which would allow them to put MBBS after their name.

Some of my friends chose to wait until the official recordings had been sent through the post. The majority of us had worried secretly about failing; if our name had been omitted from that list, grief would have to be nursed in front of our friends. However, I decided to take the risk, not wanting to prolong the agony of waiting.

There was a hard jostle to reach the front of the crowd. I stared in disbelief at my printed number alongside my name. My ambition to obtain a distinction in medicine had not been attained, but I had achieved that longed-for success. I had qualified in medicine.

I was now unemployed, and had to find two six-month posts, one in medicine, the second either in surgery or obstetrics; either of these, allied to the post in medicine, would allow me to achieve registration. Only then would I be enabled to practise as a doctor.

Marriage was not without its problems for a working woman in medicine. Hospital house posts were residential, and I would have to live apart from my beloved husband. Weekend leave was only available after every two weeks on duty, by which time I knew I would be exhausted. Generally within hospitals, junior doctors had to cover for their own wards on a twenty-four-hour basis, as well as having some evening and weekend casualty duties. I did not look forward to this change of lifestyle, as we both depended so much upon each other. I wanted to work reasonably near my parents in Acton, so that a lot of time would not be wasted in travelling homewards when off duty. I also needed a good post, one that would give some prestige to my career. I wondered if I was being over-ambitious. However, I was very fortunate. One of the Barts consultants, a physician, was also responsible for some medical beds in Whipps Cross Hospital in Leytonstone, Essex. He had been an excellent tutor and his much-coveted post for a junior houseman on his medical ward was available. I was turned down in my application for the houseman post in medicine at Barts; however, that I had anticipated, since I had only succeeded in achieving the 'Prox. Access' in the medical scholarship award. I decided to proceed with the application for the post at Whipps Cross hospital.

There were several other applicants, one of whom had already gained some clinical experience, having completed a six-month post on a surgical ward. He had every confidence of success, and seemed to think the post was surely destined for him. His self-confident style imbued me with self-doubt, but strengthened by Alan's support, I made myself apply for the post. Much to my amazement, I was given that coveted post of junior houseman within a male medical ward. My good fortune seemed almost unbelievable; surely it had been an answer to my prayers.

The staffing levels were totally different to that of a London teaching hospital. In the latter, the consultant had staff at both junior and senior level, as well as a lecturer who also undertook clinical duties. Non-teaching hospitals had only one houseman serving in each speciality; the houseman was often newly qualified. There was also only one 'middle-grade' registrar, who was normally obsessed with obtaining either his Membership of the Royal College of Physicians (MRCP) or that of the Fellowship of the Royal College of Surgeons (FRCS). Most of these more senior doctors chose to leave the routine admission of all new patients, and all casualty duties, to the houseman, thereby allowing more time for his studies. There was so often an unwritten law that had to be followed. The registrar was not to be called, unless genuine advice was essential, or there was a real emergency. This often led to stress experienced by the houseman, since sometimes a second opinion following the examination of a patient would have been of real benefit.

The situation was somewhat relieved by the appointment of a consultant in charge of casualty duties. However, at that time, I was generally rather fearful of casualty duties. I tried to learn to cope with drunken casualties, but found it difficult. Generally, there was only one other person in the casualty department to whom one could turn for help and protection if violence was threatened, and that was the female nurse on duty. Life could feel a little frightening at times.

Generally, such casualty duties were only undertaken after 5 p.m. by a houseman, one who had been serving on the ward, where he or she also undertook weekend duties. I dreaded being called up in the night following a long day in the ward. So often I would find myself staggering with weariness down the long corridor leading to the casualty department. It was there that a young drunkard bound me in his arms, crushing me to his chest. On that occasion, I was rescued by a young policeman who just happened to be present. I was very lucky.

Another time, on a late busy Saturday evening, a young man, a victim of a motorcycle accident, was admitted. Peter was conscious, and had no external injury, apart from a very slight bruising on the skin of his forehead. Following a careful clinical examination, I came to the decision that I could detect no signs of an internal or external injury. He remained fully conscious throughout my time with him, vehemently declaring himself free of pain. I did not think that any emergency investigations were necessary. I finally decided that the young man probably required further observation on a short-term basis, for which admission to a medical ward was necessary. I bleeped the houseman, that being the normal procedure, asking him to prepare for a new admission. I gave him all the clinical details regarding the patient, adding that although I anticipated his early discharge, I considered the patient would benefit from bed rest, his blood pressure being rather low. It was my firm belief that a two-day rest period would alleviate the shock that must have been experienced. I then decided to start on my examination of the next patient.

I never knew quite why a surgical registrar, one who was off duty, decided to make his way through to the casualty department at that time before departing to go to a concert for which he had tickets. It was a providential deliverance for that patient of mine. The registrar was Italian, very knowledgeable, one always willing to give advice when requested. He gave me a friendly smile, then stopped in his tracks by my still-conscious patient. I told him that Peter was awaiting admission to a medical ward. A swift examination was made.

'This man is descending into shock,' he whispered softly. 'His blood pressure is low; it will soon be down in his boots. Something must be done. *Now.*'

'I've taken blood for cross-matching as a precaution. The patient does not seem to be bleeding. He is being admitted to the medical ward for observation.'

'He is descending into profound shock. He must be bleeding somewhere. There is no time to waste, none at all, or else shock will be irreversible. He needs a transfusion *now*. No time must be wasted. I will phone the lab immediately as we will need quite a few pints of group O Rhesus negative blood.'

The blood requested was in the universal donor group, for use in extreme emergency situations. The demand for such donor blood always had to be made by a senior doctor. It was clear that I had to cancel my request for the blood that was probably already in the procedure of being cross-matched.

'The blood will have to be given very quickly indeed else there will be no time left for that young man.' Even as that surgeon spoke, he was again taking the patient's blood pressure, then gently but swiftly examining his body. My patient's eyes were closed, as if in sleep.

'Possibly a ruptured spleen. I'll let the theatre know that they have an emergency on their hands.'

I obeyed all his instructions mutely. Then I looked at the patient's arm.

'Veins are collapsed,' I muttered. 'I will never find one.'

'You can do a cut down.'

That meant cutting down through the skin tissues in order to find a vein, then making an incision through the wall of the vein, through which a small tube or cannula could be introduced. It then had to be sewn into position and only then could the blood be dispensed. I had never been taught, or even witnessed this procedure. I did not even know how to use a blood pump.

The surgeon smiled. 'I will do it, I will show you.'

'Your concert?' I muttered.

He shrugged his shoulders eloquently. Undoubtedly that surgeon saved the young man's life. In my ignorance I would have allowed him to die. It was a salutary lesson for a newly qualified doctor, one that I would never forget. Doctors must learn by experience; learn when to call a senior doctor; one who could both clarify the diagnosis and monitor the treatment of a patient. However, I did feel the system was at fault. I thought that a senior doctor should always be in charge of the casualty department, not only to monitor injured patients, but also be there to take responsibility for training junior staff in such emergency procedures.

I thought it sad that despite the fact that my helpful and highly experienced surgeon had gained the Fellowship of the Royal College of Surgeons, he never succeeded in obtaining a consultant post in this country. He subsequently returned to Italy.

Roger was another such man. He too was a very highly experienced surgical senior registrar, having gained the fellowship awarded by the Royal College of Surgeons, the FRCS. Roger was always prepared to give some advice either during a ward round or over a cup of coffee after lunch. He was such a reassuring man to have within the hospital, in which he spent most of his time as he had no family commitments. Roger had not found a consultant post; however, he always presented a cheerful face to his surgical team. One morning we were shocked to hear that Roger had killed himself with an overdose of drugs. He was found within the bleakness of the bedroom within his flat, his body stretched out upon his bed. I pictured him sitting alone for hours on end, with that black dog of depression squatting firmly on his shoulders. Roger, we all missed you so much; we should have helped you; forgive us. You were devoted to your work within the hospital; it was your life.

Chapter 9

Exhausting though it was, I really did enjoy my work on the medical ward. I have never forgotten the first patient from whom I took a history. His name was Andrew. Although still in his early thirties, he had been admitted following a twenty-four-hour period of semi-consciousness. I tried to obtain a medical history from Andrew, but with very little success. He seemed rather withdrawn, and I assumed it was due to the shock experienced following his forced hospital admission during his period of semi-consciousness. I learnt that his last visit to his family doctor had been during early childhood, following an attack of measles. He seemed very reluctant to impart any information to me, either of himself or his family. I found him to be suffering from hypertension, or raised blood pressure. Andrew's blood pressure was certainly very high; however, it became lowered following drug therapy. I had carefully discussed the correct dosage to be prescribed along with my registrar because of my inexperience in such matters. I anticipated an early discharge home into the care of his family doctor, following the successful outcome of his treatment. I then decided to concentrate all my attention on another new patient.

I had established a good working relationship with the nursing staff. The ward sister was of particular help, and spent time introducing each of her patients to me; which I found to be of great value when initially dealing with their clinical problems. I noticed with some amusement that the most junior probationer nurse within the ward seemed drawn towards Andrew. It seemed odd to me, but she appeared determined to spend most of her off-duty time alongside his bed. Andrew's speech seemed to be disjointed at times, but the young nurse, whose name was Christina, listened to him, and at times she even took some notes. Her visits during her off-duty periods were noted by the ward sister who was a strict disciplinarian. She issued a stern reprimand to the young nurse: at all times nursing staff had to preserve their professionalism. It was of no avail. Andrew had no other visitors; the visits continued, and later a vase of red carnations appeared by Andrew's bedside.

I continued to maintain pride in my work, rarely allowing myself much free time. There was so much to accomplish while working as a houseman, and at times I felt exhausted. I was somewhat surprised when during one of my really busy times, the junior nurse much criticised by her ward sister, requested some time to talk with me. She introduced herself as Nurse Christina. Initially I was reluctant, the admission of yet another new patient being my priority. However, the nurse was persistent in her request, and the introduction between us was finally made during my lunch hour. She fixed her eyes firmly upon my face while she spoke, explaining that owing to her junior status, she believed that the registrar, being the senior doctor, would place no value upon her opinion.

Looking at me anxiously while she spoke, the young nurse told me that she had been asked to admit the patient to the ward, ensuring that he was comfortable in his bed. Initially Andrew had been reluctant to talk. Following my medical examination, the young nurse had sensed that a major clinical problem had not been disclosed. As I listened in amazed silence, a new world regarding the patient Andrew was opening up before me. Lunch was forgotten while she continued to speak to me. Christina had spent most of her off-duty periods sitting by the patient's side, holding his hands, and encouraging him to talk. It seemed that Andrew had constantly declared his eagerness to return home within the immediate future. Eventually the truth had emerged during her stay by his bedside. He told her that when he returned home, he would swallow all the pills he had been prescribed from hospital and put an end to his life. This information had been revealed to Nurse Christina during the times when his speech appeared to be disjointed, the words so often being repeated. However, the objective was clear. On most occasions he had seemed to be unaware of what he was saying, his speech persistently being rambling in nature, while his face continued to express the depth of his misery.

Nurse Christina explained that Andrew's career had been that of teaching. He was the deputy headmaster of a boys' grammar school, and was currently on compassionate leave. Andrew's parents, along with his only sibling, a sister, had all died, following a recent car crash. As a family they had been very close. I expressed surprise. Andrew had never revealed any such information either to me, or to any of the senior medical staff. Apparently Andrew had already spoken with the senior registrar, expressing his wish to return home, along with his willingness to attend a follow-up outpatient appointment. This had already been organised for the patient, and a discharge date from hospital had already been agreed; this also I had not known. Andrew's sole aim had always been a rapid return home, along with the determination to end his life.

Christina seemed very distressed while she continued to talk with me. Clenching her hands together, leaning forwards while fixing her eyes upon mine, her words suddenly streamed before me. It was her belief that the doctors had spent too much of their time examining the patient, and arranging for various clinical tests. She flushed as she spoke, lowering her gaze. No one had spent any time talking or listening to the patient; even Sister had failed to establish any continuity of communication. No one had acknowledged his problem. It was Christina's opinion that Andrew was in urgent need of help.

'Please listen to me,' she said, raising her eyes to mine again. 'I am certain that Andrew is very depressed.'

I remember feeling utterly shocked at the time. It had all seemed such a straightforward medical case, not only to me, but also to the senior doctors. Medication for the raised blood pressure had been decided upon as the complete solution to the patient's problems, and no further clinical diagnosis had been considered. The young nurse, still in her first year of training, had learnt that he was presenting an urgent clinical problem.

Following consultation with my senior registrar, Andrew was transferred to a psychiatric ward where he was given the help and care he needed, and he eventually responded to his treatment. I made sure that praise was duly accorded to that junior nurse. A patient's life had been preserved. I made some final enquires, and it was my understanding that in time Andrew would be enabled to return to his teaching post. Andrew, during his treatment for depression, was eventually steered through those deeply troubled waters of grief, being guided to a safe shore, where his life could be resumed.

Using my limited medical knowledge, I had placed total reliance upon a clinical diagnosis of hypertension. As a result, I, along with the registrar, had failed to explore the patient's real needs. A junior nurse, doing what I had most enjoyed as a nurse myself, listening and communicating with her patient, had discovered the underlying problem. I vowed to use that humbling experience to shed a guiding light over the times ahead of me.

I missed Alan so much. I wanted to be close physically, to share reminiscences, to be reassured, and to express my love. The telephone was of some comfort. Alan, in the throes of his final examinations, had little physical support from his wife. Housemen were allowed to leave at 9 a.m. on the Saturday of their off-duty weekend but I always seemed to be delayed. I remember one explanation to Alan over the telephone: 'An emergency has just been admitted; my registrar is coming over to see him, and wants me to stay here in the ward, because I admitted the patient. I'm really not sure what time I'll be home.' Such conversations were not conducive to a healthy relationship.

I was so exhausted on one particular weekend that I had made up my mind that nothing must deter me from leaving the ward at the appointed time. I had been on active duty for near twenty hours. I had one seriously ill patient, and had carefully explained all his medical details to the houseman allocated to stand in for me. The wards were 'twinned', and whenever one houseman had a weekend off, the second took responsibility for all the patients in his ward as well as his own. Unexpectedly the registrar appeared. I explained that I would be away, and that all the relevant information had been passed on to the other houseman. How fiercely his blue eyes gazed at me. 'When I was a houseman, I was not expected to leave a seriously ill patient. I do not expect you to do so either.'

I had experienced a very hard time on duty for the past three weeks, along with little sustained sleep. Something within me snapped. 'I am sorry, sir: I just have to get home. It is an urgent family matter.'

I realised that I had put my career at risk; there was a possibility that my reference relating to the service that I had performed within that hospital might not be glowing as a result. I had my priorities. I needed my husband, and he needed me. Surely rest had to be a priority for the safety of the patients; my fatigue limit had finally been reached.

I learnt a lot on this particular ward. Unlike Barts, and other teaching hospitals, the patients admitted in the general hospitals tended to have 'bread and butter' illnesses, commonly detected in general practice. Our beds were filled with patients with chronic chest complaints, often induced by long years of cigarette smoking, others with problems like incipient heart failure and chronic rheumatic diseases. They were in stark contrast to the relatively obscure and more exotic conditions that on some occasions were referred to the teaching hospitals.

One weekend, my ward was 'on take', which meant that beds were available for emergency admissions. One such patient was a man in his late seventies, with a progressive neurological disease resulting in impaired speech, loss of reasoning power and increasing muscle paralysis. He was admitted from a nursing home with inflamed sores almost down to the bones in his back. His skin was in an appalling state. I tried to organise everything for him: a hoist so that he could move more easily up and down the bed, for he was a tall man; ultra violet light for the healing of his sores; antibiotics for the pneumonia I detected in his lungs. No matter what I did, the patient continued in his suffering: for him there was no relief.

My registrar and his consultant visited the ward two days later, on the Monday morning. That day I learnt a lesson that I never forgot.

'Did you not know,' said the consultant physician very gently, 'that pneumonia can be one of man's best friends?'

The cessation of all medication was ordered. A few days later, the patient died peacefully in his sleep. In the years to come, Alan and I tried to keep in mind those words 'Thou shall not kill, but need not strive officiously to keep alive'.

One of my more difficult patients was a doctor who had served in the Second World War. He was admitted with severe pain in his chest, which I thought was angina, although he appeared to otherwise be in a fit physical condition. However, I heard a heart murmur, which is an abnormal sound over the site of the heart valve.

I decided to use my initiative and take some blood, ordering some tests that I thought might clarify the situation. Carefully I took the precaution of speaking to my registrar over the telephone, since the patient was medically qualified and my status was that of a junior. My registrar monitored the drugs to be administered. On the following Monday morning my consultant paid a visit to the ward. There I received a sharp rap over the knuckles for daring to order a blood investigation termed the Wassermann Reaction, or WR test, for the doctor, especially as I had not sought his personal permission. It was at that time one of the main tests for syphilis. My consultant expressed his annoyance with me in no uncertain terms. In disgrace, I was ordered to leave his presence, thereby missing part of his ward round. As a result of this, I was asked to obtain the results of all the patient's clinical investigations undertaken in the pathology department. This task was normally accorded to a nurse.

Surprisingly the test for syphilis was positive. The infection had caused an inflammatory disease within the walls of the aorta, the main artery of the body. Apparently, after the patient's primary infection possibly some years earlier during service abroad, there had been an initial latent period where the patient had been free of symptoms. This was later followed by the demonstration of disease, during which time the normally elastic tissue in the wall of the aorta had been replaced by fibrous tissue. There had been a consequent dilatation of the aorta, followed by damage to the heart valve. The medical patient had been unaware that he was in the tertiary stage of a dreadful disease. He had to be given an intensive course of medication. I felt sad for that patient, even more so for his wife and his family.

It was not an easy situation for the consultant. He never referred to the matter again, but he certainly did his very best for me on a later job application, giving me every support. I was given a very sound reference, which was absolutely invaluable.

I decided not to undertake a surgical post for my second six months before registration. I sought one in either obstetrics or gynaecology, both of which were acceptable for registration purposes. I wanted to work in London, because of the prestige of learning in a London teaching hospital situation. I applied for every available post. In many hospitals, women did not seem to be appointed; however, I did my utmost to succeed. I dashed across the capital, having put in several applications in the hope of attaining some positive interest. I actually did get short listed in one excellent place, where I put in a bid perhaps against my better judgement. It was for one of two posts: an obstetric or surgical junior houseman. I was faced with four men at the interview. There I was told that my sex was far more vulnerable to fatigue, and less able to withstand long hours of duty. I was also informed that women could become unpredictably pregnant, thereby failing to give a sustained service to the consultant.

I knew I had to fight for myself. I had worked with other women doctors; I was aware of their capabilities, both for hard work and devoted service. I informed those interviewing me in no uncertain terms. Vivian Georgina was never one for making speeches, but that day one was uttered. The outcome was surprising. I was offered a post in surgery. It was an amazing opportunity, but some strange intuition made me turn that surgical post down. Obstetrics was my final goal.

Even at that point in my career, I was aware of the constant tension between my married life and that of my professional ambitions. I did spend time wondering whether I should forgo the latter. Love and loyalty within my marriage were surely of vital importance. I gave a lot of thought to the matter.

There seemed to be an apparently reasonable post being advertised in a small Ealing hospital. Alan's parents lived there and it was only a couple of miles from my own parents' home, where we still had our married base. Even our combined salaries did not allow us to have a separate home, since we had to pay for our compulsory board and lodging while serving in hospital.

While training at Barts, Alan had entered for every scholarship. He almost swept the board. The scholarships or prizes in surgery, obstetrics and gynaecology; paediatrics and dermatology became his, alongside medals in pathology and anatomy. I think all these awards compensated him for his initial rejection as a medical student at Barts. It certainly gave the dean, who had taken the risk of accepting him following my request, some continuing cause for amusement. Only the Kirke Medical Scholarship in Medicine eluded Alan, but then he had pressured me into some success. We had worked as a team.

Following qualification in medicine, Alan achieved the post of his dreams; that of junior houseman to Sir

James Paterson Ross, Barts senior surgeon, who was in charge of the surgical unit; the one who was also surgeon to the Royal Household.

While on one of his ward rounds, the surgeon had told us all an amusing story. One day when called to Buckingham Palace, he was initially turned away, having presented himself while using his bicycle as the means of transport. Arrival within a prestigious chauffeur-driven car was the usual mode of entry into the Royal Household. The surgeon's words were greeted with loud laughter. Learning at the feet of one of the greatest masters in surgery, Alan felt fulfilled. My husband had truly become a Barts man, albeit a humble one.

In the Ealing hospital, I had an interview with Miss Aileen Dickens for her houseman post in gynaecology. She was a consultant obstetrician and gynaecologist. Miss Dickens had not only trained at University College Hospital in medicine, but had also obtained a post there as a registrar. She seemed to be greatly interested in my nursing training at UCH. Few women at that time had managed to penetrate the consultant circle, and these in the main were those working in obstetrics and gynaecology. Miss Dickens was known for her enormous capacity for work. Like most female consultants in those days, she was unmarried; unlike most, she was a very attractive woman, and her large kindly blue eyes invited confidences. I talked to her about my lifelong interest in medicine; the anxiety I experienced that being female I would find it almost impossible to gain entry into a teaching hospital as a student. I smiled as I looked upwards into the eyes of a woman who had become acknowledged as a distinguished obstetrician and gynae-cologist. I then went on to explain just why I had initially ventured into the field of nursing, and later described my training in medicine. I found myself telling her that I did not really enjoy surgery, that I did not envisage making a career in either gynaecology or obstetrics, but felt that her post would offer me invaluable experience, which would be of particular use in the field of general practice. I made the point that most women found the prospect of a pelvic examination both embarrassing and stressful, and the majority preferred a female doctor. Doubts suddenly beset me at that particular point. Had it been wise to tell this prestigious consultant that I had no interest in a final career within the field of obstetrics and gynaecology? The interview ended at that point in time, and I became overwhelmed with the sure belief that she must have lost any interest in my application.

Miss Dickens listened to my words patiently, after which she informed me that providing the six-month period spent in the gynaecological unit was successful, there would be an offer of a second six-month post in the obstetric unit within the Perivale Maternity Hospital, a unit separated from the main Ealing Hospital, and thence from its supporting facilities. The interview then came to an abrupt end. There were other candidates for the post awaiting interview, and I was advised to wait outside until each had been seen. I felt so weary, and there seemed so little prospect for me gaining the position.

The end of a long afternoon arrived. Nearly all the candidates looked anxious, all saving one very learned-looking woman. She seemed very assured of success, and told us that she had received excellent references from a consultant physician while serving in a London teaching hospital. Her ambition in life had always been that of becoming a consultant in obstetrics and gynaecology. She assured each one of us that Miss Dickens had already intimated that she was the most likely candidate to obtain the post. There was only one male candidate. Faced with all the female candidates, he looked disconsolate.

Finally the interviewing of all the applicants came to an end. Patiently we all waited for a name to be called. Unbelievably the name called was mine, and I was offered the post, much to my surprise and joy. It seemed like a heaven-sent miracle. There was much consternation expressed by the patiently waiting unsuccessful candidates on that afternoon, in particular by the woman who had believed herself to have been selected. She expressed utter amazement at what she considered to be the most unlikely choice.

My new chief was devoted to her specialities of obstetrics and gynaecology. She enjoyed teaching, and I benefited enormously from my service in her gynaecological ward at the Ealing hospital. It was a relatively small building, serving the local population. Once inside, one was welcomed, and readily directed to the correct area. There was the usual casualty department, alongside wards serving the needs of medicine, surgery and gynaecology. There seemed to be relatively few staff on the gynaecology ward. I was the only houseman and there was a single registrar, who also was responsible for Miss Dickens' obstetric ward at her other unit in Perivale, as well as the gynaecological unit in Ealing. Miss Dickens also undertook some private work, so she had a very full timetable. In short, the junior houseman at the Ealing Hospital had a fair amount of clinical responsibility thrust upon his or her shoulders should immediate medical help not be readily available. In such an emergency, the houseman was permitted to ask one of the Ealing Hospital surgical registrars for advice.

It was a similar situation at Perivale; there the obstetric unit also faced some disadvantages being in a relatively isolated geographic area. The houseman was thus obliged to telephone the non-resident registrar when in doubt or trouble. In a real emergency, the patient not only lacked the ready availability of supporting services like pathology and radiography, but also lacked the presence of experienced senior staff, which could be life-saving both for the mother and her unborn babe, as well as the newborn infant. This could occur because the registrar also undertook service at the Ealing gynaecological unit, along with the obstetric unit in Perivale and both were far away from each other. This meant that the presence of a doctor experienced in obstetrics during an emergency situation could not always be guaranteed. There were, of course, the regular weekly ward rounds made by both the consultant and registrar. However, such geographical isolation of an obstetric unit was not, I understand, a situation recommended in later years.

The gynaecological post was very hard work, particularly as one had to undertake duties in the casualty department. I still remember one busy weekend, when a forty-year-old married woman came to casualty with an enormous abdominal swelling, claiming she was 'unable to pass her water'. She had a pelvic examination undertaken by the doctor in charge, who was of houseman status. He had suspected the presence of an ovarian tumour. During the pelvic examination, it was much to the patient's astonishment, and the doctor's chagrin, when, following the rupture of the membranous walls of the amnion, which enveloped the developing embryo, the examining couch became splattered with amniotic fluid. For some reason, the doctor had failed to feel the baby through the abdominal wall during his clinical examination, while the woman had not only failed to see that her increasing girth was due to pregnancy, but also did not understand the significance of the absent monthly menstrual periods. Her guileless response to questioning raised some smiles. 'Doctor, how should I know? Never had a baby before.'

Another patient I remember well was during my service on that gynaecological ward. A woman in her mid-twenties had been admitted as an emergency during the evening with acute abdominal pain. She was in shock, and had lost some blood.

Miss Aileen Dickens was finally summoned to the scene, and an ectopic pregnancy, the development of the fertilised egg outside the normal cavity of the uterus or womb, was diagnosed. Quickly the patient had the much-needed operation, and she slowly recovered in the ward. The patient could have died had she not come to hospital and everyone was delighted with her progress. Certainly the condition was uncommon.

The staff were advised that the husband served abroad in the navy. However, he arrived unexpectedly in the ward on the following day. I thought it wise to have a private word with him before he spoke with his wife, just to reassure him about her condition. I thought it could be quite difficult for a layperson to appreciate the dangers of a baby developing outside the womb. Carefully I explained the situation, assuring him that all concerns for his wife's immediate health were over. She was clearly on the road to recovery, thanks to our obstetric consultant Miss Aileen Dickens.

A shocked silence was his immediate response. Slowly the patient's husband gave me the facts. On arrival home from overseas, neighbours advised him that an ambulance had been seen to arrive during the earlier part of the previous day, which had transported his wife to hospital. The man's speech was vehement. He was an army officer and had been serving abroad for the past twelve months, during which time he had never seen his wife. It was not his baby. I didn't know what to do – his angry voice could be heard by others, but there was no other staff member on duty so I was left to deal with the situation on my own. I did wonder in retrospect: what should I have said to that distraught man? He departed in anger, and made no further visits to his wife. It was such a sad situation. The young patient was finally discharged, returning to her mother's home. I often wondered whether there was ever a reunion between that man and his wife. I would never know.

I proceeded to the obstetric post in Perivale after my six-month service. I was secretly fearful of a mother undergoing labour, fully aware that if forceps were misapplied during an abnormal delivery, the brain of the baby could be damaged. I used to take a pair of forceps to bed with me, along with an obstetric book, and talk my way through the various manoeuvres again and again.

During the time when we were both off duty together, Alan would be by my side, and we would practise together. It was a joy for us both to learn together. In time I felt more competent; one who could be trusted, within the limits of her experience, not only to deal with a forceps delivery, but also to understand that in certain situations, both the advice and presence of experienced help was essential. During a very difficult delivery, permanent damage to the infant's central nervous system could ensue, with the consequent loss of bodily functions; the life of a newborn baby could even be lost during such a delivery. The call for experienced help could certainly be life saving. I had a lot to learn.

There was a price to pay during those very early years of qualification. Time together for both Alan and myself was very limited. Our home was not far from my obstetric post, but while on duty, it was not possible for me to leave any patient experiencing problems, unless I had been relieved by my registrar. He could well be undertaking an operation in the theatre at the Ealing Hospital when such contact was being attempted. When Alan and I finally met together in our free time, we were usually both exhausted. Generally Alan made every attempt to pick me up at the beginning of my off-duty period, but on so many occasions, he had to patiently bide his time while I was attempting to sort out the medical problems of a patient.

Such stress was endemic in medical life. One of my friends, a very gifted obstetric registrar, who later became a professor, eventually separated from his once-devoted wife. He worked incredibly hard, and I believe that his wife paid the price. The strain for her had become intolerable.

I had a great respect for Miss Dickens, and she was extremely good to me. She had a reputation of backing her staff, once she considered them worthy. She knew that I did not enjoy surgery, and confessed that I resembled her in some respects. Suddenly one day, just after a ward round, she turned to me, and much to my astonishment, announced: 'I will stand by you if you want to carry on with obstetrics.'

I had never discussed a career in obstetrics and gynaecology with Alan. In fact, I had never given any real consideration to it. Under her guidance, I too could become a consultant. The answer was deep in my subconscious. Miss Dickens had devoted all her life to her work; however, she was unmarried.

'I want to carry on working in medicine, but I *must* have time with Alan. I want to have a family; I want children of my own.'

It was a cry from the depths of my heart. Miss Dickens smiled in sympathy; it was surely something that she had denied to herself.

'Then you must think very seriously about a career in public health. It will give you time for your family life. There is an excellent one-year degree course at the London School of Hygiene and Tropical Medicine. You must think about it, then come back and see me. We can have a talk together. I would of course provide you with a reference.'

Miss Dickens was an intensely loyal colleague and I had been incredibly fortunate in obtaining those two house posts under her service. She assured me of her loyalty, her full support; that a career in obstetrics and gynaecology still remained my choice, and I would always be backed by her lifelong support in whatever branch of medicine I decided to follow.

I promised to consider the proposition. My dream was of having a family while still working in a medical career. However, it was a truly wonderful offer but would it be right to accept it? I was yearning to be a mother and my beloved Alan would undoubtedly become a consultant surgeon, and he would surely need loving support from his wife.

Were there not some words that lingered from my days at Sunday School?

'Lead kindly light, amid the encircling gloom; the day is dark, and I am far from home. Lead Thou me on.'

I knew that an answer to my problem would surely be provided.

Chapter 10

The general practitioner was the link between the consultant and the community, and responsible for advising and treating patients following a diagnostic consultation. Patients needing specialist medical treatment or surgical intervention were referred to the relevant consultant either in medicine or surgery. Doctors trained in public health specialised in the maintenance of broad health aspects, serving both their local community and people on an individual basis. These doctors were called medical officers.

After I became qualified in public health, various clinics employed my services. The information rendered was on such factors as fitness, diet and adequate fluid intake, all of which are essential concerns in the maintenance of physical health. Education to do with health was of vital importance, and such health issues could always be discussed during the medical sessions spent either within the schools, or the local authority clinics. Later in my career, I gave talks concerning the various aspects of health education in the local town hall; I gave one regarding accident prevention among schoolchildren, which certainly received a warm welcome, and at another the dangers of smoking cigrattes was discussed.

During my training in medicine, I had been introduced to issues relating to public health in the 1950s and the early 1960s by a female friend who had previously served as family doctor. Mary had already worked within the field of public health for some years, and it had been for her a time entirely free of stress, which she also had enjoyed to the full. There were no health emergencies relating to the individual, all such problems being allocated to the family doctor, and thence to the specialist trained to serve the patient's medical needs. Public health was the ideal service in which a married woman doctor with her own children could play a part.

Medical officers took responsibility for the examination of school children (taking place within the school premises) and also that of babies and pre-school children under five, who were seen in the local authority clinics. There in the clinics, mothers could freely discuss with the medical officer any concerns regarding their children's health issues, such as obesity or food allergies. Educating my patients about health matters was an essential part of these consultations and mothers were always encouraged to ask for advice. Any medical conditions observed by the medical officer during a clinical examination, such as a heart murmur, the absence of a testis in a boy's scrotum, or suspicions concerning anaemia, were immediately referred back to the family doctor. The parents were always advised about such a referral. Sleeping difficulties and behavioural problems were occasionally noted, while general fitness problems, along with being overweight, were not uncommon.

One of the concerns frequently raised by mothers, some of whom were living alone, was that of behavioural problems with their teenage children. Unfortunately even if the family was blessed with a father, he could rarely attend, due to work commitments. Medical officers also specialised in the prevention of ill health due to other external factors, such as the dangers of lung cancer inherent in the smoking of cigarettes, alongside that of an early introduction to alcohol, which was occasionally present in the young teenager. Sadly cigarette smoking was sometimes practised by teenagers, although it often was difficult to get them to confess to it. Sexual health education also was of particular importance in relation to young people, especially those of teenage years still within the school situation.

The head of the school sometimes requested the medical officer to give a talk to the pupils, more commonly on fitness or accident prevention, and this could always be arranged. The head of the school, however, rarely acknowledged sexual health problems. My friend told me about one occasion when a local family doctor, along with herself, had been asked by the headmistress to give a talk to the school children on the prevention of road accidents involving young people. This was then followed by a session where the children were able to ask questions. The request had followed the near fatal road injury to one of the pupils within the school. The occasion had been warmly welcomed both by the parents and the local press. In ideal circumstances, it seemed that medical officers of health and family doctors could work hand in hand together, each serving to care for the community in the prevention of ill-health.

While reluctant to leave clinical medicine, I found that the idea of working within the field of public health was a tempting one. I had always, even in my nursing days, been intrigued with the challenges presented by those vital issues within health education of the general public, as well as to the school communities.

Yet despite the importance of such public health programmes, I had initially wanted to train as a physician, a specialist in the medical diagnosis and treatment of disease. Exploration within the field of clinical medicine had always been my strength and my love, while serving and learning on the wards as a medical student. The concept of leaving hospital life altogether concerned me. More importantly, it saddened my husband Alan. He had envisaged a life in which we worked together, he as a surgeon and I as a physician. The surgical training was both long and arduous. Promotion up the various rungs of the ladder, which was so essential for success, could not be guaranteed. Further examinations had to be passed. Later Alan had yet another dream: that I might possibly consider training in anaesthetics. I could then remain by his side, thereby rendering a team approach within the lives ahead of us. It was not to be.

I was in my early thirties. I wanted a family. I longed for a child of my own, perhaps even the luxury of two. We wanted a boy first, followed by a girl. I had always been ambitious; however, I knew that if I remained within hospital walls I would find no time for the joy and the luxury of family life. Working in public health offered me an opportunity to work as a doctor as well as raise a family. There was some tension between Alan and I over the final decision to be made. Alan, when qualified, had far to travel in his professional life. He was armed with many hospital awards and scholarships, including that of the Brackenbury Scholarship in surgery. In my heart I knew that much of the allure of working within public health was the fact that the time spent within such work was on the whole reasonably limited. One aimed to work within the usual working hours of 9 a.m. till 5 p.m. Another important factor was the pay awarded to medical officers. It would certainly be higher than my hospital pay, at least initially, and the hours worked not only would be shorter, but certainly would be far less stressful than those of working within a hospital, or even within that of a family doctor practice. Finally the decision was made. A training in public health seemed to me to be absolutely vital for the preservation of health and happiness within our marriage. I longed to have children of my own along with time, precious time to render loving care to my children, time to enjoy our married life; time for togetherness.

I applied for entry to the London School of Hygiene and Tropical Medicine. There, after a year involved in full-time academic studies, I could take the Diploma in Public Health: the DPH. I knew that competition for entry was intense. Able and experienced friends of mine had failed: however, I could depend upon a full backing from my obstetrician with whom I worked, and I knew that she would give me a glowing reference. My hopes were high. Surely my prayers would be answered.

Alan and I still lived in my parents' home. Fees would have to be paid for the course. I needed to have enough money to pay for the train travel up to London each day, and books would have to be bought. Again my mother and father offered their support, but I knew that there had to be a limit. Doubts assailed me. Eagerly, yet in trepidation, I waited for that vital acceptance letter through the post. It reminded me of the days when I had wanted, with every cell of my being, to become a medical student, when I then had twenty pounds in hand, saved during my nursing training. At last that long-awaited letter arrived. I read it again and again, almost in total disbelief: I had been rejected.

All my hopes were dashed. No reason for rejection was given, but I did wonder whether it could have been due to my lack of postgraduate experience. 'Perhaps,' I reasoned, 'it was meant to be.' Perhaps God had not meant me to select the pathway leading to public health. I still had my hospital appointment to finish, and in time, I would surely be shown the way ahead on which to travel. The disappointment was deep. Had I been wrong to turn down the offer from Miss Dickens? Should I have taken up a career in obstetrics and gynaecology? Undoubtedly that remarkable woman would have given me encouragement and constant support throughout my career. Doubts continued to assail me.

Basically I knew that any form of surgery, which obstetrics and gynaecology would involve, frightened me. I still had not overcome my fear of cutting into body tissues and blood vessels, which I experienced early on during my student days. Still deep within me burnt that intense desire to have children of my own, and I could not see that it would be possible for me to carry on with a busy hospital life, as well as care for my own children in the way that they deserved. I knew the sacrifices Miss Dickens had to make. She had never married but devoted all of her life to her work.

My hospital post finally finished. I had completed the hospital posts essential for registration as a doctor. Still in deep doubt, I took a locum in general practice in Hackney, and managed it single-handedly for four long weeks while the sole doctor in charge took a holiday. The practice was run from the doctor's home, which was sited in a small pleasant garden area just to the rear of the main road. It had obviously been selected with care. The waiting area adjoining the consulting room was reasonably spacious, and had views out to the garden. I was impressed with the consulting room. It was bright, and the walls were decorated with various certificates, medical degrees and diplomas. I knew that my short entry into general practice would be an education for me, one that had been entirely neglected during my student apprenticeship.

General practice was certainly not easy. I met patients whose medical background was entirely new to me, all of whom needed a clinical examination prior to treatment. It was a major challenge. The problem was that of time: as I was new to the practice, I needed more time for each and every patient. Many of those patients who came to see me were from a relatively poor background. Some of the small children I saw seemed to be malnourished; however, others appeared to exist upon food with a high fat content, but low protein value, leading to weight problems and sometimes extreme obesity. I always tried to give practical advice, and I saw for myself that health education at school, even at a young age, would surely prove invaluable.

I was somewhat concerned when one man of dubious appearance wanted me to sign his passport. I had to say no: 'I am sorry, but in order to sign a passport, I need to have known you for at least two years. As you know, I have never met you before today.'

'You will do it for me, Doc. I must have it today, now, this *minute*.'

'I am sorry. You must wait till your doctor comes back from his holiday.'

'*You will be sorry, yes, you will be. You will be very sorry.*' His tone was deeply threatening, while the lips became tightly compressed. Eyes expressed anger.

We looked at each other fixedly. I advised the man to see his bank manager.

Inwardly fearful, I watched him back slowly out of the consulting room. Later I learnt that he had previously served a prison sentence of some several years. He was known for his violent nature. I was grateful that he never paid a repeat visit, regarding myself as very fortunate.

There was no further contact with the man, in spite of his threat. It had certainly frightened me.

I became overwhelmed with demands for sick certificates. There was no one from whom I could obtain advice, and in some cases I could find no clinical reason to give one. However, I knew that many suffered appalling home conditions, and I only wished I had the time to visit each and every one of them at home, thereby achieving a closer relationship with the patient's problems and possibly coming to relate more to their family situation.

The longing for a training in those preventive medicine aspects of public health returned in full force. Many of the people who came to see me required only loving care and concern, along with some general advice, rather than a prescription. I took special care to follow up children, paying a second visit to their home whenever possible. I saw some dreadful housing conditions. When the occupants had an associated disease like asthma or recurrent bronchitis, I recommended rehousing. There were several families with whom I became involved, where parents with several children were living in small tenements with just two bedrooms. I always followed up my request to the housing department, making sure that every effort had been made to help the family. One of my most difficult tasks was often that of obtaining a bed in hospital for an acute case, particularly for those who were elderly. There was an emergency bed service available; however, it took up much of my time over the telephone, and I became very frustrated at times. A secretarial service would have saved so much of the precious time I needed to spend with my patients, but there was no such help available within this particular practice.

I remember one young man very well. His anxious mother requested a home visit during the early hours of the morning. For some reason I could detect very few abnormal clinical signs and symptoms, but I felt very uneasy, as did the mother, an anxious working-class woman, who pleaded with me: 'I'm so worried, but I don't know why, Doctor. He doesn't have much of a temperature.'

Michael, who was seventeen, just felt ill, and lay listless. Following an examination, there were no clinical signs of disease that I could detect. There was not too much I could say, but I promised to revisit immediately following my morning surgery. By that time Michael's temperature had risen considerably. There was a rash over his lower limbs, and he had an increasingly severe frontal headache. There was indeed something seriously amiss, and I really regretted not paying a second visit before the start of my early morning surgery. I did worry, knowing I lacked experience within the field of general practice.

'My neck, Doc...' groaned Michael.

That had to be a warning sign. Carefully I re-examined him. Yes, there was some neck stiffness, certainly not present when previously examined.

'There is some measles around,' Michael's mother interrupted my musing. 'Of course he had it as a boy.'

Suddenly I remembered when I was a medical student during a teaching round within a fever hospital. The consultant was smiling in triumph as we all stumbled through the various diagnostic possibilities presented by one patient; but somehow I had hit upon the correct diagnosis. Relieved by that memory, I flexed Michael's thigh to ninety degrees from the abdomen, and then tried to straighten the knee. Initially it was impossible, owing to spasm of the hamstrings. It was that clinical sign I had learnt while a medical student. I became certain that it was a condition described as a positive Kernig's sign. It made me wonder. Did Michael have meningitis? I told the mother that she had been absolutely right to call me; instinctively she had known her son was seriously ill. Should I give a shot of penicillin, and then organise admission to hospital? Ideally I knew I should wait until the infective agent was identified before administering an antibiotic; this could be undertaken within the safe conditions of the hospital environment. There what is known as a lumbar puncture could be undertaken, leading to the aspiration of spinal fluid, which could be examined under a microscope. I knew I was inexperienced. There was no one to whom I could turn. Delay could cost the life of that young man. Unfortunately, there was no telephone available within the home. There could be a delay in getting him admitted. I had therefore to take a risk: administer penicillin and then do my utmost to arrange an urgent hospital admission. A life had to be saved.

I injected a shot of intramuscular benzyl penicillin and instructed the mother to bathe her son with ice-cold water, for his temperature was rising fast. I then left, running to the nearest telephone box, which was close to the patient's home. I contacted the emergency bed service, and finally managed to gain an admission to hospital. Michael was admitted as a patient and survived. Had I not given him the penicillin, I think he would have died. This incident was one of many that made me very much aware of my own lack of knowledge in such medical matters. Family doctors had to learn to be tough, and I was still so inexperienced. I had to accept that I was still in a learning stage.

I came to dread making emergency visits to patients' homes, especially during the night. I had no idea that people lived in such poverty and squalor. On many occasions I felt bewildered and frustrated. Having found a flat after much difficulty, for some were unnumbered at that time, I would on the more rare occasions find the patient bent over the television set, either intent on watching a football match, or even a film, not wanting to be disturbed until a more convenient time. It seemed odd to me, having been called out to visit. I had always assumed that one was only requested to make a home visit when the patient felt too ill to visit the family doctor. I had been naive. Sometimes it seemed to be impossible to find a parking space near a patient's home, so during the dark hours, I learnt to take a taxi. It was a wise decision to take, while working during those dark and sometimes wet hours of the night.

One patient I will always remember. He came to the practice along with his sister; she gave me his full life history. He suffered from schizophrenia, a sad and serious mental disease where there is a failure to relate thoughts and feelings to everyday events. It seemed that his sister devoted herself to his care. There seemed little I could do to alleviate his circumstances, except to listen, but I did my best. At the end of the long consultation, the man suddenly turned to me, and said: 'You really do care about me, don't you Doctor.'

The memory of those words, and his smile, has remained with me over the years. Somehow that patient encouraged me at a time when my spirits were somewhat low. I was very inexperienced, and could only do my best, but that had to be better than nothing. Certainly I did care about each patient I saw.

It made me wonder. Did I want after all to become a family doctor, rather than serve in public health? Again I was somewhat assailed by doubts. After a month, the doctor returned from his holiday; he seemed to think I had served him well, which was comforting. It had certainly been a learning experience for me. I had, however, eventually come to realise that a family doctor service could take much time and energy. At the end of a long day, I had felt completely exhausted. I came to realise that life as a family doctor was probably not a practical solution for one who yearned for her own family life.

I recalled my friend Mary, the one who had introduced me to that fascinating field of public health in which she had worked for some two years, and it had been a stress-free time for Mary. It was at that point in time that my decision to venture into that realm became final.

Alan was disappointed: he still held out hopes that I would remain within the hospital service. However, he gave me every encouragement in my pursuit of a career in public health. Quietly one evening, he pointed out an advertisement in a medical journal. A prestigious scholarship, the Sir Arthur Newsholme Scholarship, was available at the London School of Hygiene and Tropical Medicine. The winner would not only have the fees paid while studying for the Diploma in Public Health, but a grant would also be made available for general living expenses. Could my dream come true? Dearest Alan, you cared for my happiness.

The situation seemed ludicrous. I had already applied for admission to the course in public health and been rejected. My rejection could have been on the grounds of inexperience, for many of the applicants had already attained further experience while serving the community in general practice, and others had served at a senior level within a London teaching hospital or gone on to postgraduate study. How then could I have any chance of obtaining such a prestigious scholarship?

'Try, try, and try again,' was Alan's reply, urging me onwards.

I had only undertaken two houseman posts after qualification: one in medicine, and the second in obstetrics and gynaecology. Then I had taken the 'Prox. Access' or second place for the Kirke Gold Medal in Medicine at my teaching hospital. I had also shared the first place in the Roxburgh Scholarship in Dermatology. However, all this could not take the place of time spent in general practice. Mine had been strictly limited to those unforgettable four weeks, during which I had always been conscious of my lack of experience. However, I realised that practising doctors always had to be humble; there was always something more to learn within the field of medicine.

Alan left the decision to me. It took me some time to make up my mind. The limited time period spent in general practice had been of major help. Along with my husband's full agreement, the decision was finally made. I applied for entry to that scholarship, and learnt that it basically consisted of a series of interviews. There was no written work. For me in particular, it certainly was a challenging prospect. I had never regarded myself as a good speaker; I had always lacked confidence in self-presentation. Could there a chance for one such as me?

Chapter 11

It seemed quite a few years back, but once I had worn a rust-coloured suit for my interview at St Bartholomew's Hospital and it still fitted. I had certainly aged in appearance, and there was some suspicion of grey amid the darkness of my hair; however, a recognisable image stared hopefully back at me from the mirror.

The interview was long but surprisingly pleasant. I had never thought myself to be a good speaker, being too shy and sensitive. Alan had warned me that I had to sell myself. How was that to be achieved? Strangely it seemed, my nursing training seemed to help: they seemed genuinely interested in my background. The place of women in medicine evoked much discussion. My short service in general practice proved more useful than anticipated. While a medical student, I had received no information, and no training regarding the place of the family doctor in the field of medicine; my introduction to the subject, in spite of the limited time spent in service, proved to be of great value. I found myself expressing my feelings as never before, rendering vehement viewpoints. Those interviewing me appeared to listen with interest. I felt encouraged. I was after all only a recently qualified female doctor, privileged to have been accepted for training within the portals of London's oldest and perhaps most famous teaching hospital; one who was still inexperienced within all the fields of medicine.

I left the London School of Hygiene and Tropical Medicine feeling comforted, pleased to have taken the plunge, and been given the opportunity to meet the staff and view the school. It was yet another life experience. My expectations were not high. Many of the applicants, who were in the main female, presented themselves, during that time together awaiting the interview, as being highly experienced, particularly within the family doctor service. There were only a small number of male applicants, who in the main were of recent registration.

A month following that interview, I received a letter. Alan and I, still living in my parents' home, were having breakfast. We had been discussing renting a small place of our own. Alan opened the letter. It was unbelievable. I had been awarded the scholarship affording me entry in the London School of Hygiene and Tropical Medicine at no expense to myself, I had been awarded the privilege of studying for the Diploma in Public Health. The letter had to be reread on several occasions. I had to believe the unbelievable.

In retrospect, I came to realise that the four-week period spent while serving as a locum family doctor during a holiday period had been invaluable. I had learnt a lot, and felt that the patients had not suffered unduly from my lack of experience. I had cared for their health, and while talking with them, had learnt to express myself with some force, believing that in many cases, patients needed some sympathetic guidance regarding their personal welfare, along with the acknowledgement of their importance in the role of parenthood.

The concept of spending yet more time pursuing academic studies filled me with some alarm, but it had to be faced. We decided to stay yet another year with my long-suffering parents before seeking a place of our own. Funds would be too sparse for such a venture and Alan earned little as a house surgeon. In any case, he was obliged to reside within hospital walls while on duty, so our times together were limited. I could take the underground train service into London, and make sandwiches for lunch, in order to preserve funds.

I longed to work within the community, but cannot pretend to have thoroughly enjoyed the studies within all aspects of public health; it was a means to an end, an introduction into the health problems experienced within the community. I worked very hard during the DPH course, in the realisation that I had been so fortunate in gaining that scholarship. I selected as my special subject to study the topic of mental health. It was fascinating. I had always been interested in psychiatry, but the training was for me too long and not easy for a woman. During my time at the London School of Hygiene and Tropical Medicine, I made a visit to Broadmoor. It was a humbling experience, making me recall those words uttered by my mother: 'Each one of us must remember. There but for the grace of God go I.' I saw that awareness of mental health was of vital importance, which possibly had not been adequately covered during our undergraduate training.

During my training, I realised how important the school health service was. Time was allocated within the school hours for each child to be seen by the medical officer for a medical examination, followed by time to talk to the child: the latter I felt to be of vital importance. Children could raise their worries, and we could give them guidance. Suspected medical problems, such as that of organ or skin disease, would always be referred back to the family doctor for advice and treatment; the medical officer, trained in the field of public health, never intruded upon the family doctor's role in medicine.

Each student had to write a dissertation on some aspect of public health. I selected the controversial issue of hospital versus home confinement, having gained some experience within that field while serving in the obstetric ward under Miss Dickens. I certainly held strong views on the subject. A maternity service was available, which could be called to the home in an emergency, and of course there was the availability of midwives; however, I had always felt that the hospital environment was the safest option for the mother. I could well have been mistaken, but I was also influenced by one of Alan's recollections. He would always remember being called to a home while a medical student as part of his training. During delivery, a sea of blood surrounded the mother, following which both the mother and her baby daughter died. It was tragic. The parents had recently bought their little home and everything had been carefully prepared for the new arrival. The placenta was apparently in the wrong position, and this had not been diagnosed during the antenatal period. Two lives could have been saved during a hospital confinement. This was the information received by Alan, and certainly influenced our thinking in the years ahead. My beloved husband was haunted by the memory of that lost mother and her baby for many a year.

My dissertation was accepted. I had to have it professionally typed and bound, but that was all part of the course. The final examinations for the Diploma in Public Health would arrive all too soon. I felt there was so much about which I was ignorant, and vowed never to take any more such examinations. However, I was also eligible to take the diploma in obstetrics and gynaecology, due to my time spent under my superb consultant Miss Aileen Dickens. Alan persuaded me to face the challenge; I had to 'fight the good fight with all my might'. I prayed for strength, and it came. I did at last finish the final papers for the Diploma in Public health, and following that time 'had a go' at the Diploma of the Royal College of Obstetrics and Gynaecology. Strangely enough, I enjoyed tackling both the written and practical examinations, even though I always felt the latter to be somewhat intimidating.

Hopefully I awaited the results.

with the problem. I found that laughter remained the best medicine when talking about such problems with young people. It ensured a happier relationship, along with that of trust.

In time, an easy accord followed with most school heads and schoolteachers. My work within schools became valued, and really enjoyable.

Chapter 12

Awaiting those final examination results made me feel desolate: supposing I had failed? Had I piled too much upon my plate? Sadness seized my spirit; maybe the whole year had been a waste of time. Alan and I had been separated for a whole week while he was on duty. I was musing upon my loneliness when the postman arrived with a letter. Forcing myself to open it, I read that I had gained the Diploma in Public Health. In all honesty, I do not think there could have been too many failures. The candidates were after all a collection of highly motivated mature postgraduate students, the majority of whom were female. However, the relief was enormous. I could scarcely believe my good fortune. Alan had supported me all the way. I owed it all to him.

We needed a place of our own. Although both my parents were devoted to Alan, regarding him as a son, we must have intruded upon their privacy. We found a small basement flat in Doughty Street in London. Charles Dickens had once been a neighbour, and because of that, I felt strangely honoured. Life ahead looked to be enjoyable, and we knew that we could afford the rent once I had obtained a post in public health.

I received a second letter later in the week, informing me that I had been successful in obtaining the Diploma in Obstetrics and Gynaecology. I could now proudly put the following degrees after the name of Vivian Georgina Edwards: SRN; MBBS; DRCOG; DPH. The girl who once had chosen to live in a world of dreams, was a state registered nurse; a Bachelor of Medicine and a Bachelor of Surgery; obtained the Diploma of the Royal College of Obstetrics and Gynaecology, along with the Diploma in Public Health. God had answered the prayers of a one-time dreamer.

I forged ahead and applied for a post as a medical officer in the borough of Wandsworth. I was successful. It seemed unbelievable as it was the very first post for which I had applied. I knew I was in a very privileged position. The pay was very reasonable, the hours were strictly limited to those of the day, and I looked forward to working among infants and young people. A new and challenging life lay before me.

It was a totally different world. There was stress of sorts, but none of the hurry and scurry experienced within hospital life. There I had so often suffered feelings of inadequacy and incompetence while working within my junior status. I was constantly aware that any clinical decision taken could compromise the health of the patient, or even cause the loss of a life. While junior doctors, when in doubt, could obtain the advice and guidance of senior doctors, usually a registrar, this could not always be made available on an immediate basis. Sometimes the senior doctor would be performing an operation or be engaged with another patient. I had so often felt isolated and vulnerable, more especially while working on night duty, being constantly aware that any clinical decision made by me could be detrimental to the health of the patient, particularly so when newly admitted. Junior housemen lacked the clinical skills and the experience so essential for the complete care of the patient. Despite always doing my utmost to provide a careful clinical assessment, I lived in the realisation that I could have made a misdiagnosis.

Once, when serving as a locum junior houseman in surgery, I had been instructed to undertake an emergency removal of an appendix in a small child. I had never been left unsupervised on any other operative occasion, and certainly never before removed an appendix, even in an adult. However, I had seen the operation undertaken on two occasions, so was not entirely ignorant of the procedure. Nevertheless I felt fearful, and seemed unable to clarify the situation with my registrar as he was busy elsewhere. He advised me over the telephone what I should do. I felt forced to go ahead with the operation. During the induction of anaesthesia, the child started to vomit. It was a danger sign. Respiration could be impeded, and the child could die. Vomit could be inhaled into the windpipe, in which case either of the bronchi, the two forks of the windpipe connecting it to the lung, could become blocked and the child could become suffocated by his or her own vomit. The anaesthetist did not fill me with confidence, firmly stating his wish for me to continue with the procedure, despite my protestations. He seemed to be very sure of himself; nevertheless, I felt very unhappy with the situation. However, the anaesthetist continued to express his reluctance to abandon the anaesthetic. I did wonder: was it I who was lacking in trust? Should I start the operation regardless of my concerns? Never before had I even assisted in operating upon a child; surely I was putting my patient at risk?

I knew that *I* had to take the final decision. 'It is not safe to proceed,' I finally announced very firmly, putting down my scalpel; frankly that was said with an enormous sense of relief. The little patient would surely survive. Fortunately there was no further vomiting, and the child appeared to settle. Again I tried to obtain the immediate services of my surgical registrar with no success. The little child was operated upon two hours later by a senior surgical registrar from another ward. He assured me that in view of my operative inexperience, I had most certainly made the correct decision in choosing not to proceed, and hearing that was a great relief. There were no further complications, and the young patient soon recovered from the procedure. However, that ordeal caused me a great deal of anguish. Supposing I had been instrumental in causing the death of that little child? The system seemed all wrong. It was my opinion that junior doctors should never be left to deal with such difficult issues. Perhaps part of the problem was that I was working within a local hospital. Senior medical staff were not always readily available because of other duties, and the consultant, in so very many cases, was also not available for services within the hospital during night-time. Some sixty years onwards, when this account is being written, such conditions must surely have improved.

My first post within the field of public health entailed being in charge not only of mother and baby clinics but also antenatal clinics, along with responsibilities within the school health services. Those seen were generally in good health. Decisions had to be taken, but there was never that possibility, inherent within a hospital situation, of either death or disability following a mistaken clinical diagnosis by an inexperienced doctor during the hours of night. I learnt a lot about babies, and always enjoyed talking to toddlers; their mothers often expressed their gratitude for the advice and guidance given, which was always reassuring. I really enjoyed communicating with schoolchildren, though I still remained somewhat in awe of head teachers, remembering the bullying techniques of one particular head during my own early school days.

One amusing incident stands out clearly. The administrator, by mistake, sent me to a boys' school, where the head was known to dislike the presence of women doctors. I was not aware of this until after my arrival at the school. There I was led to a large room where the head remained seated at an imposing desk some six feet in front of me, while I examined the boys. His eyes remained firmly fixed upon me while I worked. However, I enjoyed an easy relationship with those boys, and we spoke very quietly together. The close presence of the headmaster surely must have embarrassed his pupils, for some clearly wanted to discuss personal problems with me.

I always performed a full medical examination on pupils within a school. I felt that to be essential. While a medical student, I had palpated a swelling in the breast of a young male. This was surely a very rare event. And of course there could always be a potential problem with non-descended testicles. I had in the Child Welfare Clinics, and over a period of time, found two young boys with only a single testicle in the scrotum, and again contacted the family doctor, so that referral could be made to a consultant. There are normally two testicles sheltered within the scrotum, the bag of skin carried between the legs of a male. Each testicle, the male reproductive gland, produces both sperms and the hormone testosterone, without which fertilisation of the egg produced by the female could not ensue. The lesson I had learnt from the young man and his dog, back when I was a nurse, remained with me. Since the testicle can be manipulated from within the abdomen to the relative safety and coolness of the scrotal sac during an operative procedure, it would be negligent to omit undertaking a full clinical examination. In consequence, I examined all the boys, giving to each a full explanation of the procedure. Even though I had my back to the headmaster, I could feel his scowls that he directed to me. The lads treated me with great respect. There was no awkwardness or embarrassment, in fact, many seemed grateful once I had explained my reasoning behind the procedure. One even wanted a private interview with me. I was concerned; the headmaster's close presence seemed to prevent that possibility, and no screen was available. In consequence, the young teenager spoke in a whisper, so that even I could barely hear his words. He had been mocked by his peers for the small size of his scrotum, and in particular, that of his penis. He seemed very distressed. I managed to take him to one side and we sat together while I chatted about girls having similar problems regarding their breast development, explaining that there were always such problems experienced during puberty. I assured him that he was perfectly normal, and we parted on friendly terms. The frown furrowing the forehead of that headmaster was quite visible once I had turned back to face him; I gave a smile in return. I would not be deterred, even by his fiercely frowning face.

The headmaster made a special request in a letter sent to my administrative office. Never again would he tolerate the presence of a female doctor examining any of his male pupils within the portals of *his* school. I was apparently banned for life. I always looked back in laughter when remembering that particular headmaster. It was a useful experience meeting up with his pupils. I enjoyed their company, and I believe they valued the advice that I was able to offer them.

I will always remember the actions of one particular headmistress. A young girl of near sixteen years of age asked me for a private interview. I was allowed to speak to her while behind closed screens. We both talked very quietly to each other, and the girl was almost in tears. The frightened lassie had missed one menstrual period, and acknowledged putting herself at risk with a sixth-form boy. I made arrangements for her to have a pregnancy test, assuring her that it would be without the knowledge of the teachers. I did tell her that both her family doctor and her parents would be contacted, and with that she was content; the relationship with both was good. The school nurse was very kind and sympathetic, and sat alongside the girl, holding her hand. However, I did not realise until later that either a teacher or the head had somehow managed to overhear the conversation between us. Someone must have crept up behind the screens, and listened to our whispered conversation. The betrayal of confidentiality frankly horrified me. Within an hour of my departure, the youngster had been hauled up to the head's office, and suspended from school, presumably on the assumption that she was an undesirable influence upon the purity of her peers. I eventually reported the matter to a senior medical officer; however, she decided that no further action could be taken in the matter. I felt very concerned for that young girl; further suffering had been added to her situation, and it saddened me. I contacted the family doctor over the telephone, and he expressed sympathy; however, there was no further action either of us could take regarding this particular issue. He advised me that he would undertake follow-up appointments with the young girl.

I came to wonder at a later stage: should I have reported this serious breach of medical confidentiality to the chief medical officer, going above the senior medical officer's head? It must have caused the girl considerable anguish and emotional pain, which could have seriously affected her life in the years ahead. I felt that in some way I had let her down. She was finally asked to leave the school for good, even though it transpired that the girl was not pregnant. Surely she should have been spared expulsion.

I wondered about that girl over the years. Did she feel that she had been betrayed by me? The school expulsion episode must also have caused great concern to the parents of that young girl, one emerging into those uncertainties of an early adult life. Undoubtedly they would have shared her suffering, along with their concern that her future work plans could be compromised. Their daughter had achieved good grades following her O level examinations, and there had been plans for her to continue with science studies in the school sixth form. Surely it was possible for that teenager to continue studying for her A levels at another school? I comforted myself, certain that the parents would find a solution to their daughter's predicament.

A problem that I occasionally observed both in boys' and girls' schools was that of an allergy to gluten, which can be found in wheat, barley, rye, and oats. It results in disease of the mucous membrane or mucosa of the small intestine, and is a problem that occurs worldwide, being more common in northern Europe. It can affect peoples of all ages, including infants, some of whom can present with severe symptoms of food malabsorption, while others less affected develop anaemia, become tired, and lose weight. The severe form of the disease is called coeliac disease. During my working periods within the school health clinics, I detected two girls, both aged eleven years, whom I thought to have the problem of gluten allergy, along with three boys of around the ages of twelve to fourteen years, all of whom had the milder symptoms of gluten allergy: tiredness and anaemia, and with some, a loss of weight. Each of the affected schoolchildren was referred back to their family doctor. The exclusion from the diet of gluten contained in wheat, oats, barley and rye remains essential to those suffering from these symptoms. Gluten-free bread, along with other such food products, has been available in many of the major food stores throughout the UK for a number of years. Parents can be reassured that once the gluten allergy is recognised, symptoms will be relieved, providing there is a strict adherence to diet. However, it remains a problem, which is not so easily solved among teenagers; once among friends, and outside the safe discipline of the home environment, some can become tempted by the luscious food offered by their friends. I learnt, along with a smile, to give such a warning to any pupil affected

Chapter 13

Life seemed to proceed relatively smoothly. I was enjoying the family orientation of my daily work. Alan was working very hard. The life of a house surgeon, especially in the competitive environment of a teaching hospital, was bound to be both busy and stressful. Alan studied hard for his primary examination for the Royal College of Surgeons, spending most of his time working in the surgical wards. Sometimes I saw very little of my husband; he had, however, longed to be a surgeon since boyhood. Alan had no difficulties with academic work, and it seemed to me that there was a kind of magical quality within his hands. He had a highly creative mind, which somehow seemed to avoid stress during emergency situations. He always managed to cope with surgical emergencies: he was a born surgeon. There was, however, one particular occasion when I saw him outwardly affected by a profoundly sad situation, and that was some years later.

A schoolboy aged eight years had been given a bicycle on his birthday by his parents. Somehow he had managed to persuade his mother to let him ride it to school with the promise that he would keep strictly to the pavement. However, he decided to dare entry into the busy main road. The boy swerved into the pathway of a lorry. Alan said that he found it almost unbearable to witness the grief shown not only by the parents, but also by the lorry driver. An ambulance had arrived within a very short time, but the little lad died on the operating table from his injuries. Alan wept in the comfort of my arms on his return home. We both agonised for the unremitting grief suffered by the parents for the loss of their only child, the anguish of the guilt-ridden mother, along with the emotional pain suffered by the lorry driver.

In spite of all the hard work, we both began to enjoy ourselves. Our flat was small, but it was pleasant, and I made every effort to please the landlady, who lived in the flat above us. She suffered from varicose veins, and under instructions from Alan, I made sure that her legs were correctly bandaged on a regular daily basis. I was determined to keep our basement flat, still proud of the fact that Charles Dickens had once been a near neighbour. As a child, I had become engrossed in his books, thinking he must surely be one of the finest writers the world has ever known.

My parents had by this time retired to a house in Eastbourne, and for them I think it was one of the happiest periods in their lives together. My sister had married a loving Methodist minister, and had one daughter, while my younger brother had married a sweet church friend of my husband Alan, who had made the initial introduction. In time, they had two sons, the eldest of whom trained in medicine, becoming a family doctor. We all took turns in visiting our parents in Eastbourne. There Alan and I spent our holidays, enjoying their exquisite garden, of which my parents were very proud. It was for us a very happy period. In time, Alan learnt to take holidays, rather than refusing to leave his patients. We spent much of our free time rambling together over the Eastbourne Downs, these being very near to my parents' home. It was there within the greenness and the glory of the Downs, listening to the ceaseless crying of the screaming gulls winging their way above the deep blue of the sea, watching the frothing cream of the crashing waves, that our beloved son David Gareth was conceived.

There we were surrounded by the flash of white rabbit scuts scurrying here and there with restless energy within the green beauty of the grassland. Life was unutterably sweet. The sky above us was a pale blue, flecked with the fluffy whiteness of clouds. The sward beneath us was like velvet. The air smelt fresh and sweet. There was glory around, and it was a day of happiness, one of ecstasy for both Alan and myself.

I somehow knew that I had been blessed; that I had conceived; some five weeks later, this was confirmed. I did after all have some knowledge regarding the signs and symptoms of pregnancy. It was a wonderful event, and another shared ecstasy. Motherhood would be mine. Only one who had passed through that experience would even begin to understand that feeling of wonder and joy.

I knew it would not be an easy time for both of us. Alan had still to make his way up the promotion ladder, his ambition being to become a consultant surgeon. Further examinations had to be passed, and even when attained did not necessarily mean that one was automatically promoted. There was fierce competition over the selection for such a post, especially within the walls of a teaching hospital.

Alan worked diligently, achieving a reputation for skilled surgery. He showed care and concern for each and every patient. I continued with my work within the field of public health. The chief medical officer took my news of the pregnancy well. I promised to carry on as long as possible, for I had built up a happy and sound relationship within each of my clinics. I did not want to let anyone down. I decided not to give our happy news to my somewhat awesome landlady in the top flat. I went on to purchase what was then termed a 'swagger coat', which I thought would successfully shield her eyes from my ever-increasing girth. It was voluminous, having no belt. Fashionable at that time, it was worn with pride.

My one-time chief Miss Dickens became both my counsellor and friend, the consultant in sole medical charge of my pregnancy. I developed toxaemia; my blood pressure rose, and I retained fluids abnormally, becoming what is termed oedematous, this being the pathological retention of fluid within the body tissues. Quite wrongly, I became obsessed with carrying on with my duties, failing to report to Miss Dickens those early signs of toxaemia. It was really very foolish. However, during a visit to her clinic, Miss Dickens made me see sense, suggesting I took sick leave. I had been unfair to my unborn babe, putting his or her health at risk, as well as that of my own. During that very difficult period, Alan exhibited amazing patience and tolerance towards his stubborn wife. I was by then in my sixth month of pregnancy. It was a humbling experience.

Arriving home after a further visit to Miss Dickens, I negotiated the steps to our basement flat with some difficulty, longing for the peace bestowed within our sanctuary. It was a paradise, the place where I could rest my weary feet, enjoy the peace within my little home, and rest awhile. It was not to be. During my absence, the landlady had gained entrance. She had a key, since she claimed that she needed ready access to read the gas and electric meters on a regular basis. All the clean and well-polished pieces of furniture had vanished. In their place were stained and scruffy replacements: no longer was it homely and inviting; no longer did the air within the flat smell sweet, and a somewhat sour smell pervaded. There, during the last week within that seventh month of my pregnancy, I wept for the first time. Copious tears did nothing to extinguish the misery. Why did she replace our furniture? Had that landlady observed me surreptitiously as I climbed up and down those steep steps leading to our basement flat, silently mocking my obvious attempts to conceal my pregnancy beneath the twirling skirts of that bright blue swagger coat? My spirits had taken a sudden dive. Churchill's black dog of depression settled upon my shoulders, gripping them tightly. My precious baby was not welcomed by our landlady.

It was early in the evening. Would Alan be in the operating theatre and could I somehow reach him? I needed my husband. Fortunately I only interrupted Alan's session with a dictating machine. He listened patiently, promising a speedy return home. Peace filled me that night as he lay sleeping beside me: a comforting peace that filled me with strength. I knew then that somehow we would be given the means to manage. We were not alone.

A solicitor advised us that we could take no legal action. It seemed quite clear to us that we had to move but where and when? Who would give a home on a low rental basis to a pregnant female, one within reasonable distance of Alan's place of work, St Bartholomew's Hospital? At the time it seemed to me to be a problem that could never be solved.

One evening following that disastrous episode, Alan returned back from work unexpectedly early, bearing a bottle of champagne. His eyes were gleaming merrily, but he refused to give any immediate explanation. Excitedly I sat down at our supper table. It seemed that Alan had successfully operated upon a lady with severe varicose vein problems. Quite by chance he met her a week later, in the outpatient department. Intuitively she had sensed his sadness. Alan told her about the housing problem. She smiled happily. Unbeknown to Alan, she was a member of the housing committee responsible for the selection of families on the available council housing list. Apparently applicants to the council who were junior doctors were always given priority as they had always to remain readily available for their patients while on hospital call. A small terraced council house had just become available and we could move in within a month. My illness, and Alan's position within the hospital, gave us a priority rating. It was for each of us a miracle.

The new abode was the height of luxury for Alan and me. We had two bedrooms, one of which Alan converted into a nursery. Our previous rented flat had but one bedsitting room, beset by spiders. Our neighbours were wonderful, kind and friendly. Mary and John introduced us to the various facilities, including a communal washing machine area. Previously I had to use a local launderette. Mary had a sweet little girl of her own. In the realisation that I would later have to return to work, for we needed the money, I asked Mary if there were any good local nurseries.

'Would you trust me to look after your baby?' she offered.

Surely our guardian angel was hovering above us; one who was our constant guide and shield.

I was quite ill during the latter part of my pregnancy and had to be admitted to hospital before my due date. Miss Dickens arranged for me to be delivered within Perivale Maternity Hospital, where I had served under her as an obstetric houseman during my pre-registration period. I knew the staff well, and could comfortably relax. My first labour contractions were initially painless, and I felt ecstatic. Soon I would be a mother; it was a miracle. Following that initially peaceful period, some complications arose. Alan was with me all of the time. I do not know how I could have coped without his presence, he was both my comfort and my strength.

It was an abnormal presentation: my baby's head was large, like that of his father; it was also sited in the wrong position. A very difficult forceps delivery followed. David our son suffered no injury during his delivery; for us all, and for David in particular, that was the major issue. Assurance was mine. I knew that all would be well; and that all would end well. Our baby was so very precious. Delivered by my obstetrician Miss Aileen Dickens, our son was safe. Once again I had been blessed.

Chapter 14

The arrival of our son David Gareth was an absolute joy for both of us. I nurtured him carefully, trying hard to compensate for the miserable time I had given him while in the womb. Slowly but surely he gained in weight, and quickly reached the normal milestones in development.

I will never forget David's first smile. It came within the second week of his life, and was a smile directed at me. Overcome with joy, I clasped him to my breast. He smiled both at me and at his father well in advance of the expected developmental time. An early smile was said to be a sign of high intelligence. Certainly he seemed to be a very attentive baby, one needing company and play at an early stage in his development. I became sure that his brain cells had not been starved of oxygen either during my pregnancy, nor at the time of delivery. It was not until many months later that I came to realise that my friend and obstetrician Miss Aileen Dickens had suffered the same worries as had Alan and myself, regarding the possible failure of normal brain development following any oxygen deficiency which could occur during a difficult and prolonged delivery. We knew that her superb obstetric skills had preserved the life of our baby; without her presence I think that there was a real possibility that our beloved son David would not have survived, or alternatively have suffered brain damage due to the lack of that vital supply of oxygen.

David became the joy of his grandparents. He was not the easiest baby to rear, always on the alert, and constantly needing stimulation, even during the long hours of the night. During those dark hours, he would chuckle happily, and enjoy a further feed, always secure in the knowledge that he was never alone. The baby who at birth seemed to resemble an inmate of a concentration camp, steadily increased in weight, always wanting to constantly attract my attention during his waking hours. He was our beloved gift from God.

David always seemed strangely sensitive to his surroundings. I used to wheel him round the streets of London when I was free from work; this in the main was during the weekends. I always carried him clasped close to my chest when entering our church; once inside, his cries for constant attention would cease. Eyes opening wide, he would gaze around himself in wonderment. I felt that it was a sense of mystic awe. Once we returned to the streets, he would again claim my full attention. Even when Alan was on surgical duties at Barts, I would always carry our son along to the Sunday church service; it was very close to our home. Our church was small, and was a place where one could peacefully spend time in contemplation, and abide in prayer. The church became open in the week when a church warden was available. There I truly felt blessed. Quietly David would lie in my arms, his eyes intent upon the beauty of the colourful glass windows. Later his eyes would close in sleep.

I really enjoyed David's company, even just following his birth. Eventually I had to return to my clinics. I enjoyed the work, and we needed the money. I found motherhood served to make me far more understanding of the anxieties expressed by some of the mothers with their newborn infants. Prior to the birth of David, my knowledge had in the main been gathered from those times spent within the clinics, when I met up with mothers and their babies and small children. Following my pregnancy, I became much more involved emotionally with the mothers, both in the understanding and the sharing of their joys and sorrows, their anxieties and fears. My clinics grew in size, and on some occasions, the father managed to attend along with his wife and baby. They were always made very welcome. I enjoyed motherhood, along with all those attending my clinics. It was a privilege, one that could be shared with others.

I used to keep a careful check on each attending child's developmental progress, in case there had been unsuspected brain injury during birth. The age at which a baby starts to smile is of importance during such assessment. The average age for a smile to be shown is around four to six weeks, a baby with learning difficulties generally starts to smile some time later. It could be delayed till around four months in an infant with Down's syndrome.

Most young infants can walk without help at around fifteen months, though there can be some variation in the timing. There is one particular child that remains an evergreen memory. I was sitting quietly at my desk one day just before the start of a baby clinic, when a smiling African lady entered the room carrying a baby boy. He was, she told me, nearly ten months of age. He was a bright bonny baby, and gave me a beaming smile. Suddenly the mother placed him on the floor, backing away from him, laughing all the while. Instantaneously this infant ran back towards his mother, in perfect control of his limbs. I joined in with the happy laughter. The mother showed me his birth certificate. He was indeed just one day under the age of ten months. I was saddened when the family moved to another area. I so wanted to keep in touch with that mother and her son, to observe that infant's rapid development and his progress during early childhood. Never before that time had I seen such an early physical development, nor have I witnessed one since. It was such an extraordinary experience. I still smile when the memory comes to mind.

My David became a sturdy little lad. Alan's great passion was for sailing, and our early holidays together were always spent either river or sea sailing. A restless infant, David was always soothed by the sound of rippling waters. Alan too found that activities while on water totally absorbed him, allowing him relaxation from the trials and tribulations experienced within the life of a hospital. It was there that his spirit achieved freedom, becoming one with the wind. Yacht sailing on the seas at Eastbourne became his passion during those rare off-duty periods.

I was certainly not very competent in a yacht, though I too enjoyed the soothing sound of waters rustling beneath the boat and the constant cries of the birds flying above our heads. These David loved to see; uttering joyful cries, raising his arms, watching intently, while some swooping low above our heads paused awhile, then soared ever upwards towards the blueness of the skies. We became immersed in this simple world. It was on such a holiday together that our beloved daughter Amanda Jane was conceived.

I had always been interested in the derivation of names. 'Amanda' is taken from the Latin, being translated as 'lovable', while that of 'David' was the Hebrew name of the second king of Israel, meaning 'beloved'. The biblical David, with his great love of Jonathan, those characters in the Old Testament, had always been a favoured reading of mine. I never forgot the account of the anguish expressed in David's song following the death of his beloved Jonathan while in battle. I wanted our son to be like the biblical David.

Following the birth of David, I had a dream; that I would have a daughter. I just wanted one more baby. During my second pregnancy, I had made sure that I rested well, for I still had a very labile blood pressure. Again I was under the care of my friend and obstetrician Miss Dickens. She undertook the delivery. My daughter also had to be delivered along with the use of forceps, for she too had a large head, resembling that of her brother David, and also that of Alan, my beloved husband. I believe that the expertise of Miss Dickens preserved the health and probably even the life of our daughter during the stages of her difficult and somewhat prolonged delivery. Again I thanked God that the birth had been placed in her hands.

All went well; Amanda was from birth a sturdy contented child, unlike her restless brother. He was never content to lie still. However, I had no problems with our dearest daughter. My dream had come true. She smiled and she gurgled, stealing people's hearts with her chuckles and smiles. She was always a happy infant. Unlike David, she slept peacefully throughout the night. David and Mandy, as we called our daughter, got on so well together, and our son David, being eighteen months older, lovingly kept his eyes upon his sister. I judged myself to be the most fortunate of females. My husband loved me, and I had two dream children, a boy and a girl, who were both a blessing. What more could I desire? Love ruled my life.

Chapter 15

I had breast-fed both of my babies until each reached the age of fifteen weeks, secure in the knowledge that this would boost their immune system. I wished that it could have been for a longer period, but a return to work was required, the finances being essential to our family well-being.

Following the recommendations of a nationally recognised paediatrician, I had always suggested to mothers that whenever possible, breast-feeding should be continued for a reasonable period, even up to twenty-four weeks if this were at all possible. This was in order to maintain the baby's resistance to infection, the more common examples being those of gastroenteritis and respiratory disease. A more prolonged breast-feeding period also reduced the possibility of infants being admitted to hospital for treatment following any such infection, thereby being a major factor in protection of their body's immunity to disease, both in infancy, and even, I was advised, in their later life. Breast-feeding was also considered by some specialists to reduce the risk of breast cancer in women; these were some of the health education issues that I presented to mothers during the time they spent along with me both within the infant welfare and the antenatal clinics.

It always made me happy while listening to these mothers, to hear that they actually enjoyed breast-feeding their baby; especially so when some had initially come to the decision to institute bottle-feeding. It was understood that breast-feeding could cause some discomfort to the mothers, but eventually most enjoyed the added intimacy experienced between themselves and their newborn baby. Certainly during my own times of breast-feeding, I felt enfolded in a cloak of peaceful contentment; the joy of motherhood. I only wished that I could have done so for a longer period; like many of the mothers seen in the clinics, I too had to make my return back to work.

Initially, I had somewhat reluctantly returned to full-time employment, having really relished the times spent along with David and later with Mandy, following their delivery. It had been a tremendous break from the regular routine of the work within those clinics, this in spite of the fact that the time spent there had always been enjoyable. My clinic work did not start until nine o'clock in the morning, the finishing hour being five o'clock, which worked very well for me. My clinics generally were not too far distant from home, which meant that I spent relatively little time on travel during the day. Once my daily work was completed, I could then collect David and Mandy from my next-door neighbour Mary, thereby giving her some time alone with her small son before preparing herself for a supper and restful evening along with her husband. We usually had time for a short happy chat together before I returned to my home. David and Mandy enjoyed the companionship of Mary's little son, and the three played happily together in the later stages of their development. Once my daily work had finished, I used to watch them both chuckling and playing happily together within my friend's home. I always enjoyed taking my children home. My neighbour Mary never had any problems relating to their care during my working day, and I considered myself to be so very fortunate in having her as my neighbour.

David seemed to revel in his sister's company. He always seemed so protective towards Mandy, while she responded to his presence with smiles; both laughed a lot, and played so happily together. During my working week, I always looked forward with joyful anticipation to the weekend ahead, when time could be spent with my two children. I had no clinics on a Saturday morning; all were reserved for the working week. Normally Alan had some surgical duties over the weekends, although on occasions he had at least one free day. Certainly our small home was proving itself to be both a place of peace and happiness. When my husband was still at work, I devoted myself entirely to my two children during the weekends. It was often tiring in nature, especially as they grew older, when both wanted to explore the outside world; however, we always continued to have happy times when together. Both were a daily joy in my life.

I think that for the very first time since qualification in medicine, I felt relaxed and rested. No longer was I committed to those long wearing hours on duty while working within a hospital, along with the fears so often suffered when a new patient was admitted on an emergency basis. I felt as if I had entered an entirely new world following the acquisition of the Diploma in Public Health. I felt privileged while serving in that field, and my physical and emotional health reaped the benefits of this. Life became truly enjoyable, even while at work. The health of each child was of vital concern to me. I felt relaxed in mind, and fully enjoyed the presence of mothers and their babies in the Infant Welfare clinics, along with those of the young children within the Child Welfare clinics. I also regarded discerning the health of the schoolchildren as a special responsibility. Each and every session was a pleasurable experience. It was my understanding that both the mother and medical officer worked together as a team, the sole aim being the child's maintenance of health, with the consequent happiness both within the home and school situation.

As they grew older, David and Mandy continued to influence my understanding of that vital importance for a loving trusting relationship between parents and their children. I always enjoyed spending time with the young pupils within a school. During one school medical session, I met up with a rather grim-faced middle-aged woman along with her small son, whose name was Patrick. I advised the mother to let her little son sit by her side and play, while she spoke to me. Her forehead was furrowed with frowns, and I sensed she had a serious problem. Her small seven-year-old son had already spent nearly two years in school, and according to his teacher, little or no educational progress had been made. Patrick was a restless child; his speech became incoherent at times, and he refused to make any attempt to progress either in reading or writing while at school. Private tuition within the home had been paid for by the mother, but her son stubbornly refused to cooperate. The tutor had eventually been dismissed.

I sensed the mother was of an over-anxious disposition. It transpired that she had attended university, obtained a first class degree, and anticipated that Patrick, her only child, would follow in her footsteps; this apparently was her main concern. She was a single woman, having obtained a divorce from her husband when her son was five. I listened quietly while she explained that once her son was home from school, her time was devoted solely to his tuition. However, there remained a persistent refusal on his part to make any attempt to read or to write. Apparently no playtime was accorded to her son during his time at home, this being the punishment for his misdeeds. The end-of-term school reports had been consistently poor since the time of admission, and there had been a suggestion of expulsion, this being on the grounds that her son's behaviour during the class sessions was constantly disruptive, causing disturbance among his class mates.

Patrick appeared to be a sullen little lad; physical examination revealed nothing untoward. Initially I wondered whether it would be at all possible for me to give any help to either the mother or her son; both could certainly be referred back to the family doctor, who would most probably refer the matter onwards for more specialist advice. I asked the somewhat unwilling mother to seat her somewhat restless son upon her knee while I pondered over the matter. It seemed strange to me at the time, but my sympathies were geared towards the small boy. Smiling, and grasping his hands, I directed my face towards him while I spoke. I started off by telling him that when I was his age, I used to love listening to my mother reading me a story just before I went to bed each night; that on each birthday and also on Christmas day, I would be given some lovely little story books as a reward for my good behaviour.

Patrick's face slowly turned towards me; it was a face with a glimpse of a smile. It was a magical moment. I told him to sit quietly, and to look at my picture book while I spoke to his mother. I always carried a couple within my case, along with a small teddy, just in case of need.

Patrick turned his head towards the book, initially fixing his eyes upon a picture of a stationary train within a small railway station. Each of the passengers was loaded with brightly coloured bags bulging with gifts; one young lad carried a small Christmas tree. Patrick continued to turn the pages. Surprised, the boy's mother turned to me; she had not anticipated her son's ready response to my directions. Patrick sat quietly, concentrating upon turning over the pages of the book, pondering over the pictures displayed; one held his attention for a full five minutes. It was that of a jolly-faced Father Christmas clasping a huge box to his chest; it was bearing a label with the words 'A present for my son'. I sensed that the boy was near tears. He looked distressed. I did wonder: had his thoughts turned to the father who had left him so unexpectedly at that early age of five?

My advice to the mother was firm. I suggested that all forms of tuition within the home should be put aside. Patrick must be allowed to relax once school had finished for the day and she should allow time to join her son in play on a daily basis, making him feel comfortable when at home. This should be followed by a time spent together for light meal. Apparently her son was left alone while eating; she told me that his appetite had always been poor. Tuition before bedtime had always been enforced by the boy's mother. My voice remained firm while I spoke: Patrick should be allowed to invite a young friend to tea on occasions. It was always good for young children to get together, and enjoy a play period. I finally made a firm ruling. Once settled comfortably in bed, a short story should be read to her son, perhaps even two, before he settled down to sleep. There should be absolutely no attempt to force Patrick to read during this time; the enjoyment of listening must be the main issue, and one that I believed would provide the healing touch. Something within me strongly sensed that my plan would provide the solution to Patrick's problem.

I watched with amazement when eventually the mother turned to her son. She placed him on her knee. Turning her face towards him, she set out her new plan. That very day both would go to their local bookshop and there Patrick could choose a big story book for himself. Each night, just before sleep, he could select a story to be read by his mother. Her action surprised me. I had not anticipated such a ready response to my wishes. Sensing it might take a little time, I felt that a loving and understanding bond would be built between both the mother and her son. Once that was established, I believed that

Patrick's interest in reading would be aroused; that in time he would participate in the learning process because of his rising desire to read while on his own. All this I explained to the mother; she slowly nodded her acceptance, and we agreed to meet again at the end of the following four weeks.

I did wonder at the time if I should have referred the disturbed boy back to his family doctor. I had never before during my clinic sessions experienced such a problem. This I thought had arisen because of the early bullying techniques employed by the mother in her desperate attempt to enhance her son's reading and writing abilities.

In four weeks' time, Patrick, along with his mother, paid me another visit. Smiling, he set himself before me; there was a large book clasped within his hands. It was opened, and he started to read. The words were relatively simple, and not all were correctly read; however, immense progress had clearly been made. Patrick's interest in schoolwork had at last been aroused. His mother spoke to me with a smile. She had taken my advice, spending some time by his bedside, often continuing to read the story until his eyes closed in sleep. She would leave the book by his bedside, and had always found it clasped close to his chest during his sleeping periods. Once awake in the morning, he could be observed with the book open before him, happily attempting to read aloud to his teddy bear, which always lay snuggled by his side.

Remarkable progress had been made by both the mother and her son. He was no longer disruptive within the class situation, and his reading abilities had rapidly improved. Patrick's request to join the local children's library had been followed, and his mother was clearly pleased to present her son to me during our clinic session together. It was an experience that was happily remembered in the times ahead. Patrick later became proud of his progress both at home and within his school; he became a popular boy with his classmates, and in the time that followed, a member of the school football team.

I always enjoyed my school health service visits, especially when made just before Christmas. During that time, the pupils always seemed cheerful, doubtless looking forward to the holiday ahead, along with all the celebrations, which of course included the anticipation of Christmas presents. One school I visited always stands out in mind. It was small, which was a pleasant change. I had attended it previously, and had been impressed with the courtesy expressed by the teachers, their friendly manner, along with the cheerfulness of the children. On my second visit, I came to realise that the atmosphere had changed. There was a new headmistress. She had laid down a strict rule: no Christmas presents were to be given to the teachers by the schoolchildren. This was absolutely forbidden. It had apparently been a very popular move among the pupils in the previous years. Each of the school children had donated some pocket money, which was collected by each class captain, being designated to buy a Christmas gift for their teacher. A potted plant was on most occasions the gift presented. Apparently all the children had been eager to donate. The disappointment was great. I was given this information by one of the mothers during my second visit to the school. However, she left me with a smile set upon her face. It made me wonder.

I had quite a number of mothers along with their children to interview and examine; all were children within the same class and all seemed well with each of the young pupils; that is, until I came to the last to be seen. The mother presented herself alongside her daughter, who was under the age of ten years. I sensed there was a problem. Martha, the little girl, managed to smile at me, but the mother looked anxious, and fixed her eyes firmly on my face as she sat down. Nothing was said, and I proceeded with the clinical examination after my initial introduction. Martha seemed somewhat shy, and to ease the embarrassment I put my stethoscope into her hands, inviting her to listen to the air entry in her lung fields. I found this manoeuvre usually worked well, especially among the younger schoolchildren. Martha smiled happily in response, and I proceeded with my examination. She seemed a healthy little lass, I reassured the mother. I came to the realisation that her worries remained. Looking directly into my eyes, she silently mouthed the words: 'I want to see you alone, now, please.'

There was obviously a problem, so I smiled at Martha, telling her to wait outside in the corridor, until she was called in again by her mother. She smiled happily as she left. Martha's mother held her hands tightly together as she spoke.

'My sister died of cancer, womb cancer when she was young. Just ten days ago my Martha had a bleed. It stopped after three days, but it frightened me. She is only nine years and seven months old. I've heard that cancer can be a family problem. I feel sick with worry. Will she need an operation? Please tell me what to do.'

I smiled in return, keeping my voice low. 'Martha's breasts have started to develop, that you must have noticed. I believe that Martha has experienced her first menstrual period. Certainly she has started to have her periods at a very early age. I have known this to happen with some young girls that I have examined in other schools. It is rare, but it does happen. There is nothing to be worried about, that I can promise. Martha is in very good health; she just happens to be commencing maturity at an early age.' Smiling, I held my hands over hers while I spoke.

There was silence; then tears flowed, tears of joy and relief. I continued to reassure Martha's mother, advising her to see her family doctor if she felt she needed a second opinion. There was a happy silence. All seemed to be well. Martha was recalled, and reassured. Happily she clasped a teddy within her hands. As the mother departed through the doorway, she turned her head towards me. I heard the faint whisper of words: 'Thank you so much. That was the best ever Christmas present for me and for my Martha, the best ever.'

I had then finished my work for the afternoon. I mused over that mother's words as I collected my books. It was good to have lifted the painful burden off her shoulders. I decided to write to the family doctor, and make him aware of the situation, just in case further reassurance was necessary.

My work for the day was finished. Once outside the examination room, I was met by a smiling teacher.

'You are needed in the classroom,' she said smiling. 'It will not take much of your time.'

Somewhat puzzled, I followed her back into the classroom; there she bade me sit at the desk facing the class, one normally occupied by herself. The children looked expectantly at my face while the class captain rose to his feet. He was carrying a pot of flowering orchids, which he presented to me, along with a large Christmas card, signed by each of the class pupils.

'Thank you for coming again to see us,' he said, smiling. 'Please will you come again next year? Happy Christmas from each of us.'

The class clapped in response to his words. Initially overcome with surprise, I gave my thanks, promising to do my best to return the visit in the following year; that the final decision unfortunately did not lie in my hands. Laughingly I then raised a question. 'I thought you had been forbidden to give presents?'

A voice from the back of the classroom gave the answer. 'Yes, we can't give presents to any of our teachers, but you are only the doctor, so it must be all right.'

I joined in with the laughter that echoed around the walls of the classroom.

I was overcome with amazement; never before had I been presented with a Christmas gift. The flowers were really beautiful. I intuitively sensed that the presentation was an act of defiance against the new headmistress, and I wondered how she would respond, once she had become aware of the fact that her strict instructions had been disobeyed.

Once I had returned back home, I thought of little Martha and how she was experiencing menstruation at an early age. I also thought back to my childhood – I remembered the fright and bewilderment experienced by so many young friends following our evacuation at the start of the Second World War. Placed in new homes, many were ignorant concerning the coming maturity of their body and the advent of menstruation, so that the onset of vaginal bleeding was for them both a frightening and embarrassing occurrence; neither was it an easy situation for their teachers, being unused to giving advice on such a personal topic. I clearly remember two teachers telling me that they felt incompetent when trying to deal with such matters. Health education on these vital issues should never be overlooked.

I became of the firm belief that all matters relating to health education should be introduced in the classroom, starting at the age of five. Even at this young age, it must include education on some sexual matters. Young children, in particular, need to be aware that certain parts of their body are private, and must never be touched inappropriately. Once made knowledgeable about the private parts of their body, I believe that children would be far more likely to seek advice should they feel that their privacy has not only been invaded, but their bodies have been abused. Child abuse is often shielded under a cloud of secrecy by the victim, and needs to be exposed. In my experience, which was relatively limited but stretched over the years, I learnt that young children in particular were unwilling to impart such information.

Older children must be made aware that sexual intercourse between a male and female should, in an ideal situation, only be performed by those in a truly loving and permanent relationship. Following my work within school health clinics, I came to the realisation that many young people had not understood that serious infections could be the result of sexually promiscuous behaviour. Young people must be educated in such matters: their current and future health is important not only for them but for the community, and in the future, for their own children.

Health education is a fascinating field, encompassing wide horizons and embracing many topics. It is a learning process which can in theory commence at an early stage in the life of the child, depending not only upon the physical and emotional maturity of the child, but also upon the caring and teaching abilities of the parents.

Accident prevention will always remain a vital issue. Toddlers taken on their first walks can be introduced to safety issues in relation to both pavements and roads. In the school situation, the management in the use of bicycles, in particular upon the roads, remains an important issue within the field of health education. Maturing children need instruction regarding the harm accorded by the use of drugs and alcoholic drinks which sadly have made their way into the lives of some young people even within school. Obesity is yet another health hazard becoming more prevalent among people of all ages. It is a problem that must be firmly faced within the school situation. During school medical examinations, I have done my best to both help and advise overweight young people being mocked and bullied by their classmates; in some the suffering was great. I even met with two young obese teenagers threatening suicide whose lives were only preserved by counselling and transference to another school. I found that most young people were happy to listen to talks given concerning the intake of healthy food, always being eager to raise questions following class tuition. The talks I was requested to give on accident prevention were always welcomed both by the schoolchildren and their teachers. School medical officers were always reliant upon school heads for requesting class tuition on such health education issues. In my experience, tuition regarding education on sexual matters, although offered, was not welcomed by most heads of school.

There is much to learn, and much to be understood, all of which must be made available to the maturing children while within the school situation: the preservation of health, both physical and emotional, is of vital importance.

It is my firm belief that tuition in health education should only be undertaken by specialists, those who have undergone a specific training in the rendering of those vital health issues inherent within the field of health education; such learning surely plays a vitally important role in the lives of the younger generation. I had made the suggestion during an earlier period in my working life, but the proposition had been ignored at high level. Currently personal, social, health and economic education (PSHE) is taught within schools at both primary and secondary level, but by teachers having no specialist skills in the topic. Surely it is a topic of prime importance that has been neglected.

I always did my utmost to give guidance to each mother and child during my clinic times, but I knew this would never suffice. Class involvement with tuition involving the field of health education surely remains the only logical way forward. Pupils learning within the school situation will one day become parents; those entrusted to guide their children along that pathway leading to health, both of the mind and the body. Educational advice and guidance on health matters will surely always remain an essential issue: one which I felt to be so frequently ignored.

Perhaps the proposition to include health education within the school curriculum, being delivered by specialists in the field, will be reconsidered in future times. It remains an issue of increasing importance. I think that young people in these modern times are becoming very much more independent, being far less under the disciplined control of their parents than in previous times.

However, I do believe that there would be a positive response to such tuition if taught by those fully trained and experienced within the field of Health Education.

I decided, after a lot of thought, and discussion with my husband Alan, not to apply for promotion when it was suggested. I would miss the personal contact both with infants and young people, becoming much more involved with matters pertaining to health administration. The joy I found within the local authority clinics, along with those of the school health service, would become lost. I would certainly miss my personal contacts made not only with young people, but also in the case of babies and small children, with that of their mothers. I had become enriched with their life experiences, while mine, along with my medical knowledge, could give guidance on health issues, in particular when problems were presented. Although I always recognised the importance of the correct application of administrative procedures, nevertheless, it was the patient who was always central to my interests, whether as a nurse or a doctor.

I never regretted the decision to undertake a nursing training before that of medicine, alongside my venture into the field of public health. My work within nursing and medicine had served to promote my understanding of patients. I felt myself to be in a highly privileged position during my medical service.

Together with Alan, and our two children, David and Mandy, we were united, a happy family, one for which the future was bright. I thanked God for enabling me to render service to young people, along with babies and their mothers. It was a time of happiness.

Acknowledgements

I would like to express my very sincere thanks to Charlotte Cole for her constant encouragement throughout the writing process; her ready advice and guidance along the way has been priceless. Susan Pegg, my editor at Ebury Press, also extended her helping hands, for which I am so very grateful. My gratitude is also expressed to Robert Smith of the Robert Smith Literacy Agency, who pointed me to the pathway of Ebury Press; his guidance was invaluable. My daughter Mandy and grandson David have been my continuing support and source of strength throughout the writing process. Truly I have been blessed throughout the whole procedure.

About the Author

Vivian Georgina Edwards, SRN, MBBS, DRCOG, DPH, or Georgie as she is known by her friends, was born in 1927 and grew up in Acton. She trained to be a nurse at University College Hospital, before studying to become a doctor at St Bartholomew's. She also worked at Whipps Cross Hospital where she is pictured above (second from left), spent time in general practice in Hackney, and later built a career in public health. Today, at eighty-five years old, Georgie lives in Lewes, East Sussex.